DERBY COUNTY

The Rams in Europe

Andy Ellis

The History Press

First published 2012
Reprinted 2019

The History Press
97 St George's Place, Cheltenham,
Gloucestershire, GL50 3QB
www.thehistorypress.co.uk

British Library Cataloguing in Publication Data.
A catalogue record for this book is available from the British Library.

ISBN 978 0 7524 6216 5

Typesetting and origination by The History Press
Printed in Great Britain by TJ International Ltd, Padstow, Cornwall.

Contents

Foreword

For those of us blessed to be working for the Rams, particularly during the 1970s, those electric nights of European football will forever live in our memory. To be fair, even during the early days of the Brian Clough reign, Europe was a distant dream with the exception of maybe the odd pre-season tour to Germany or Holland. Nobody in their wildest imagination could have predicted the buzz, enjoyment and pride that everyone connected to Derby County felt as we began to pit ourselves against some of the finest club sides from the Conitnent. Not only did we play against the best, we actually beat the best, and in some cases outplayed the best entirely due to the fantastic quality of the squads that Brian, and subsequently Dave, assembled. The Rams were embarking on a remarkable journey which would have a profound effect on the lives of all fans who followed them home and away.

In those days UEFA rules dictated that qualification to the UEFA Cup was restricted to one club per city, causing great consternation among the clubs in London, Liverpool and Manchester. However, in those days only the champions of the respective leagues entered the European Cup and that is as it should be. The ridiculous idea of extending places to teams finishing, in some countries, down to fourth was madness and purely driven by the greed of UEFA and the unbelievable arrogance of some 'big' clubs who considered they had a divine right to play in the competition, irrespective of whether their results merited it.

From someone who in the early 1970s had never flown outside the UK, the prospect of travelling to major European destinations was what dreams were made of. Truly we had been privileged at the Baseball Ground to witness some of the greatest players of that era play for the Rams, and they in turn were becoming household names in Europe – Derby County was being mentioned in the same breath as the likes of Real Madrid, Ajax, Benfica and Bayern Munich – not bad for a club which less than ten years previously had been a moderate small-town team performing in Division Two.

The solid sliver galleon presented to the Rams by the Real Madrid president should be in prime position at Pride Park to remind all those involved some thirty-five years on just what the Rams can achieve; oh for those heady days to return so that new generations like us can taste those magical moments!

For a young man making his way in football administration, the opportunity to travel to countries offering such a variety of cultures and witness my team play against the best in Europe was an amazing experience. It is difficult to recount all the highlights as there were so many, but I count myself extremely lucky to have been in the right place at the right time.

Michael Dunford
Assistant Secretary to Chief Executive, Derby County 1970–94

Introduction

Derby had been playing foreign opposition for many years in various friendly matches before, as reigning FA Cup holders in 1946, they were invited to play all over Europe. However, as the Rams' decline of the late 1940s and early 1950s saw them relegated to the Third Division (North), the opportunity to play these foreign clubs disappeared, especially as the club could not afford to invite such teams to Derby. However, the introduction of floodlights in the 1950s meant that midweek friendly fixtures could take place and it was the Scottish clubs that featured heavily in those.

The three main European club competitions were out of reach for Derby until Brian Clough guided them to the League Championship in 1972. Their participation and winning of the Texaco International Cup gave them an insight in to the methods of two-legged matches and they launched their first assault on the main European trophy during the 1972/73 season. As one of the leading English clubs in the early and mid-1970s, Derby County took part in the European Cup twice and the UEFA Cup twice, before competing in the revived Anglo-Italian Cup tournament for three years in the early 1990s, reaching the final in the first year.

Rams fans patiently wait for an opportunity to join Europe's elite clubs in competition again – although participation in the Champions League is not realistic, their best way of getting back is to win one of the two domestic cup competitions. It has been thirty-six years since their last appearance in the European Cup, yet as at July 2011 Derby County were ranked in 140th place (when the original European Cup format is combined with the Champions League format) or 75th (when the competition was known as the European Cup). The source for this is the UEFA Champions League Statistics Handbook, published by UEFA, Geneva.

I'd like to thank Andy McConachie of www.derbycountyprogrammes.co.uk for the loan of the programmes, John Ellis for correcting the grammar, the football clubs who all gave permission for their respective logos to be used and also to Michael Dunford who was one of the few people to have been involved throughout all of the various competitions from the inside in various roles from Assistant Secretary to Chief Executive.

And I wouldn't be forgiven if I didn't mention my wife Jenny and daughters Naomi and Katie.

Anglo-French Friendship Cup 1961/62

This strangely named competition was only held twice, in 1960/61 (when it was called the Anglo-Franco-Scottish Friendship Cup) and 1961/62 seasons, and it followed an unusual format where the competing teams were not playing for themselves, but for the League against their counterparts. Teams would play just two games against a French team on a home and away basis and the trophy would be awarded to the League who scored the most points over all the games.

There were many of these Friendship Cups around Europe in the late 1950s and early 1960s – French-Italian, Swiss-Italian, Benelux and a Spanish-Italian – but they all gradually faded from the European football calendar with the establishment of the major competitions such as the European Cup, European Cup Winners' Cup (from 1960/61) and the increased size of the Inter-Cities Fairs Cup (later UEFA Cup) from 1961.

In the summer of 1960, the French Football Federation decided to organise a competition that would have four representatives from England and Scotland (including big clubs like Celtic and Liverpool) playing against eight French teams who had not automatically qualified for the major European club competitions. Participation was based on league position, with clubs selected from the two top divisions. Even at this early stage of the competition there were arguments – originally, the format was of all the British clubs competing under the one umbrella; however, the Scottish League objected to this and so two trophies were produced. As a result, at the end of the first tournament, the two competitions were separated from one another. The National Football Museum has in its possession the National Liaison Cup of Football Leagues 'The Friendship Cup': The Football League v The French League, one of the few reminders of this forgotten competition.

Derby were not invited to play in the first year of the tournament but it was decided at a board meeting in July 1961 that an application be made to be considered for the 1961/62 competition and by the end of September the draw had been made.

L'Association Sportive de Béziers

11 April 1962
Derby County 1–0 L'Association Sportive de Béziers
Derby County: Matthews, Barrowcliffe, Conwell,
Webster, Moore, Hopkinson, Hall, Havenhand, Curry,
Parry, Roby
ASB: Hairabédian, Daure, Sieber, Griffiths, Bourdel,
Goudard, Canal, Lubrana, Cristol, Saez, Boukhalfa
Referee: Mr Windle (Chesterfield)
Attendance: 6,987

After the draw Derby originally proposed that the home leg be played in October and the return game in France played in April, at the end of the season. By mid-November Derby still had not received any response from France and wrote to the Football League asking if they could withdraw from the competition. The League refused this request but with their assistance the dates had been fixed by the end of December. The visitors were captained by Welshman Bryn Griffiths, who had been playing in France for several years and actually had a one-game trial with Derby way back in 1951.

Derby's form since the turn of the year had been abysmal, with just one win in the previous 12 games – a 4–1 victory over Bristol Rovers at the end of March. That poor run had seen them slide from fourth place in Division Two down to a mid-table place with just five games to play and only five points above the relegation places. Liverpool were top of the table with Leyton Orient in second place.

ASB's form was not much better with just one win in the previous six matches and were in seventeenth place and just one point off the bottom of the table. The Easter weekend games had just been completed (a 2–0 loss at Scunthorpe United on Friday and a 4–0 defeat at Huddersfield Town on Monday), so this was the third game in a busy six-day period. Manager Harry Storer made two changes from the Easter Monday game bringing in Conwell and Hall to replace Davies and Stephenson; this could have been an opportunity to try out some more of the reserves in what was nothing more than a friendly against a foreign team.

The pre-match view was that the French side did not have a chance and it would be a matter of how many goals the Derby forwards would score. The visitors were all amateurs relying on full-time jobs away from the football club to make a living. Despite showing a lack of confidence that comes with such a long time without a win, the game was largely dominated by Derby. Jack Parry had the first good attempt at goal, when his header in the thirty-sixth minute produced an acrobatic save from the French keeper Hairabédian.

Ron Webster was making only his fifth first-team appearance and, playing in a right-half position, he was probably Derby's star performer on an otherwise forgettable night. He was instrumental in the only goal in the sixty-seventh minute – firstly breaking up a rare French attack and getting the ball back to goalkeeper Reg Matthews and then running forward from the clearance to take a pass from Jack

Parry on the left wing before squaring the ball the wrong side of the defence to the oncoming Bill Curry who scored easily with his left foot.

The main player in the ASB team was the Welshman Griffiths whose father had taken the rare opportunity to see him play. Griffiths played in front of the back four defenders in what the local press called a 'Tottenham-styled tactical retreat' – his sole aim was to break up play before the Derby forwards had a sight of goal and not to stray upfield. The *Derby Evening Telegraph* reported that 'his positional play was perfect, his distribution often immaculate and his concentration ice-cool.'

Only twice was Reg Matthews called into action, the last being five minutes from the end of the game when a double save from Saez and then Sieber kept Derby in front. The real stars of the game were the ASB defence which held out so well, especially as they had to play for the last forty minutes with their left-back limping and being a passenger in the team (substitutes were not introduced until the 1965/66 season). Despite this good work, for most of the game they left Don Roby in lots of space, unmarked. He was so out of form, however, that he posed no real threat

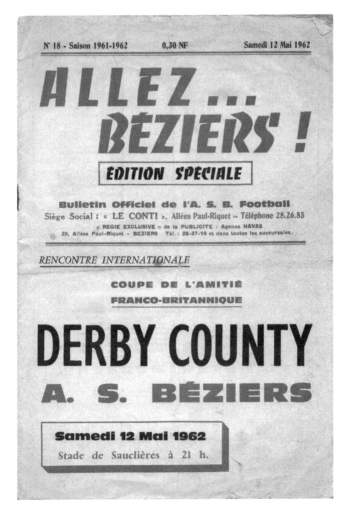

The French programme from the away trip to Béziers.

and with the other midfield players, Havenhand and Hall, also suffering a lack of confidence, Bill Curry was left isolated up front.

The French press said that is was a magnificent result for ASB and 'they fought with energy and all their faith.'

12 May 1962
L'Association Sportive de Béziers 2–1 Derby County
ASB: Hairabédian, Lavagne, Facerias, Griffiths, Albert, Goudard, Lubrana, Saez, Diouf, Leandri, Boukhalfa
Derby County: Matthews, Davies, Conwell, Webster, Moore, Hopkinson, Hutchinson, Havenhand, Curry, Parry, Roby
Referee: Mr M. Rios (Nîmes)

The ASB team showed five changes to the team that played in the first game and had won their last two matches against Aix and Cherbourg. Derby's league form had not improved since the first game, winning just one of the remaining five games, a 2–0 victory over bottom of the table Brighton & Hove Albion. That game was on 28 April, a fortnight before the game in France.

While in France, Derby were trying to arrange a further two games in an end-of-season tour, but nothing was finalised. The players and management flew from Derby airport to Toulouse on Thursday 10 May and would return on the following Monday to allow the directors and players to attend the Supporters' Association annual dinner on Tuesday. While in Béziers they were based at the Grand Hotel.

There were still two weeks to go in the French domestic season with ASB in the relegation places and in desperate need of points; they had to wait until a win on the final day of the season to escape relegation.

There are no records or match reports for the game itself, the final score being 2–1 in favour of the home team and there is no record of the Derby scorer. The overall winner of the competition was the English League, winning by 10 points to the French's 6 points; the results looked like this:

Division 1
4 December 1961 – Blackburn Rovers 3–1 Nancy
1 May 1962 – Nancy 1–0 Blackburn Rovers
13 December 1961 – Lens 2–4 Cardiff City
7 March 1962 – Cardiff City 2–0 Lens

Division 2
13 November 1961 – Southampton 2–1 Bordeaux
1 May 1962 – Bordeaux 2–0 Southampton
11 April 1962 – Derby County 1–0 ASB
12 May 1962 – ASB 2–1 Derby County

Texaco Cup 1971/72

Top Ten Division One, 1970/71

Team	P	W	D	L	F	A	W	D	L	F	A	Pts
Arsenal	42	18	3	0	41	6	11	4	6	30	23	65
Leeds United	42	16	2	3	40	12	11	8	2	32	18	64
Tottenham Hotspur	42	11	5	5	33	19	8	9	4	21	14	52
Wolverhampton Wanderers	42	13	3	5	33	22	9	5	7	31	32	52
Liverpool	42	11	10	0	30	10	6	7	8	12	14	51
Chelsea	42	12	6	3	34	21	6	9	6	18	21	51
Southampton	42	12	5	4	35	15	5	7	9	21	29	46
Manchester United	42	9	6	6	29	24	7	5	9	36	42	43
Derby County	42	9	5	7	32	26	7	5	9	24	28	42
Coventry City	42	12	4	5	24	12	4	6	11	13	26	42

Originally called the International League Board Competition, the American petroleum giant Texaco put up £100,000 of sponsorship money to rename the competition and help promote their recent purchase of the Regent filling station chain in the UK. It involved clubs from England, Ireland and Scotland that had not qualified for European competitions through league placings or cup competitions. This was the second season of the competition and sixteen clubs (six from England, six from Scotland and four from Ireland) were invited. As can be seen from the top ten table, automatic qualifiers for the main European competitions were Arsenal, Leeds United, Tottenham Hotspur, Wolverhampton Wanderers, Liverpool and Chelsea. With the League Cup competition now compulsory, Manchester United, Southampton and Everton declined the invitation leaving Derby, Stoke City, Coventry City, Manchester City, Newcastle United and Huddersfield Town as the competing teams from England.

The format of the competition was a perfect opportunity for the club to organise trips, for the management to try out new styles of play and also to get to grips with the psychology of the two-legged matches as used in the main European competitions, where they hoped to play in the future. Derek Dougan, who helped Wolverhampton Wanderers win the first Texaco Cup, agreed that the competition was a perfect introduction to 'the experience of the home and away tactics of Europe, and it was a first class rehearsal.'

Derby were already working closely with Texaco; an arrangement set up during the 1970/71 season, with large parts of the stands having Texaco boards adorning them, in what was the most lucrative deal of its kind ever negotiated by a league club.

The first round was to pair the English and Scottish teams together with the four Irish teams playing each other. Derby were drawn against Dundee United.

DUNDEE UNITED

First round, first leg
15 September 1971
Derby County 6–2 Dundee United
Derby County: Boulton, Webster, Robson, Todd,
Hennessey, McGovern, Bourne, Durban (sub Walker
45 mins), O'Hare, Hector, Hinton
Dundee United: Mackay, Gray, Cameron, W. Smith,
D. Smith, Henry, Watson, Reid, Gordon, Rolland,
Copland (sub Devlin 77 mins)
Referee: Mr G. Hartley (Wakefield)
Attendance: 20,059

There were no advanced ticket sales for the game with payment by cash at the turnstiles being preferred. Prices ranged from 30p on the Popside terracing to £1 for the best seats in the B Stand and Ley Stand. Sammy Crooks, one of Derby's all-time greats, was guest of Dundee United and sat in the 'away' directors' seats at the Baseball Ground as the guest of Duncan Hutchison who was also a former team-mate of Crooks at Derby in the early 1930s and was now a director at Dundee.

Derby were still undefeated in all competitions and had beaten Stoke City 4–0 at the weekend which put them in second place, two points behind Sheffield United. There were three changes from that team – McFarland was out with an ankle problem and Gemmill and Wignall were carrying knocks so were rested. Hennessey, McGovern and Bourne were their replacements, with Hennessey (of whom Clough said, 'he's as good a defender as we have got') appointed as captain.

Derby with such a strong side out were expected to win comfortably, but were given an early scare when after nine minutes Ron Webster's back pass was underhit and Copland was presented with an opportunity to chip over Boulton but instead blasted wide. Had they scored then the result may have been different as just three minutes later it was Derby that took the lead. Hinton got past the left-back Cameron to cross the ball to O'Hare who flicked it over the goalkeeper for Durban to nod into an empty net at the far post. The pressure on the Dundee goal was building all the time and Hinton nearly extended the lead when he volleyed narrowly wide before Hector headed in another Hinton cross at the near post on twenty-five minutes. The game and tie could have been over by half time, but Bourne had two shots off target and another that drew a diving save from keeper Mackay before an O'Hare header was saved. Just before the break, Dundee almost pulled a goal back when a Rolland shot beat Boulton but bounced off the post to safety.

Derby spent most of the first half pushing Dundee back, and it was clear to see that the Scottish defence was struggling to contain the Derby forwards. The goalkeeper did not instil any confidence by his indecision on Hinton's well-placed crosses. The Rams were cruising through the game and more positive strikes at goal and more urgency would have made the margin of victory even greater. The manager would surely have said as much at half time with Derby winning 2–0.

All the INSIDE stories

INSIDE this issue—news of a Derby County record, a Brian Clough forecast that came true, John O'Hare at home, Tony Waddington on Derby County and Colin Todd. Always in THE RAM—latest team news, Roy McFarland and Brian Clough columns, Promotions news, Ram Pin-up (in colour). All the inside stories, for you and about YOU. Make sure you get your copy, on order from your local newsagent or from a Club seller before the kick-off. And now there are tokens, too.

the Ram 7p

Official Newspaper of Derby County F.C.

No. 6 (v. Dundee United, September 15, 1971)

HELP US HELP YOU—POLICE

THE POLICE had a job on their hands before, during and after Saturday's local First Division 'derby' game against Stoke City—and once again came out of the fracas with great credit, writes DAVID MOORE.

Inspector Trevor Kitchener, supervising Pop-side control at the Baseball Ground, described some of the scenes as 'the worst I have seen in my 14 years' attendance at Derby County matches.'

There were three arrests before the game, two for being in possession of offensive weapons and the other for spraying paint from an aerosol can, and six inside the Ground (threatening behaviour, and assaults on the Police). Several spectators were ejected, and one youth was taken to Derbyshire Royal Infirmary with head injuries following a fall.

'Obviously, the fact that this was a 'derby' match heightened tension,' commented Chief Superintendent Harry Shelley afterwards.

And he issued this appeal to all regular supporters through THE RAM: 'Please keep well away from any trouble spots, even if it means waiting behind a few minutes for the Ground to clear. Some spectators do this, and it makes our job much more easy.

'If you become involved in a melee, however accidentally, it is possible that you may be jostled by Police when they take action. Should this happen, please accept our apologies in advance.

'I have known bystanders be knocked down, fortunately without injury, during a struggle. The only answer, as I say—KEEP WELL CLEAR.'

THREE BACK FOR RAMS

THREE changes by Derby County for tonight's Texaco Cup first-round first-leg game at home to Dundee United (7.30), plus one positional switch.

Roy McFarland (ankle), Archie Gemmill (thigh) and Frank Wignall (back), the latter pair having been nursing injuries, are out, and Terry Hennessey, John McGovern and Jeff Bourne—he wears the No. 7 shirt, as he did in a couple of games last season—come in.

Alan Durban switches to inside right, and Jim Walker is substitute.

'We very much want to win this competition, and the changes definitely do not reflect a lack of interest,' says Brian Clough, Manager of the Rams. 'I'm likely to bring in Terry at any time, because he's as good a defender as we have got, while John McGovern is' even better than Gemmill or Durban at marking up and winning the ball.'

Team: Boulton; Webster, Robson; Todd, Hennessey, McGovern; Bourne, Durban, O'Hare, Hector, Hinton. Sub.: Walker.

GOALS galore in Dundee United's match on Saturday, when they visited rivals Dundee. They scored four—but conceded six. United stars line up for THE RAM. Left to right—Back: Jim Cameron, Alex Reid, Alan Gordon, Hamish McAlpine, Donald Mackay, Walter Smith, Tommy Traynor, Billy Gray. Front: Andy Rolland, Denis Gillespie, Kenny Cameron, Joe Watson, Doug Smith, Jim Henry, Morris Stevenson, Davie Wilson.

The Ram   The Ram

DERBY COUNTY

2

Voucher

OFFICIAL NEWSPAPER AND PROGRAMME

Programme for the Dundee United home game.

Durban picked up a dead leg and was replaced by Jim Walker at half time and he scored within a minute of the second half starting. A good ball forward by McGovern found Hector who pulled the ball back for Walker to stroke it past the helpless goalkeeper. Within five minutes of the second half starting the tie was effectively settled as O'Hare made it 4–0, scoring after an exchange of passes between himself and Hector. Straight from the kick-off Reid punted the ball forward into the penalty area, and as Boulton came out, Gordon ran through the defence, who were guilty of ball-watching, and headed over him – we had now seen three goals in five minutes! Despite Gordon's goal, Derby continued to relax and this, coupled with the confidence given by scoring, gave the visitors their best period of the game as they settled and made some attacking moves. This added confidence was rewarded on the hour mark when Rolland collected a knock-down from Gordon, turned and saw his shot bobble past Boulton into the far corner to reduce the arrears further. Giving away two soft goals was taking the shine off an otherwise excellent team performance, especially as they had not conceded a goal in the previous four matches.

Some stern words from the dugout eventually had the desired effect on 73 minutes when Hector again was the provider for Hinton who ran on to his flick and slid the ball past the advancing Mackay. Dundee were now running out of steam as Derby's class and accurate passing were again causing problems. The scoring was complete eight minutes from time when left-back John Robson ran the length of the field leaving players behind and the defence retreating in front of him. As he approached the penalty area he unleashed a shot through a crowd of players that left goalkeeper Mackay unsighted and the ball ended up in the net.

The *Scottish Daily Express* reported that 'United were bewildered by their opponents' speed and skill and rarely looked likely to emerge with the sort of score which could be reversed in the second leg.' The 6–2 final score made qualification for the second round of the competition almost certain and the sponsors would be pleased with the attendance of 20,059 that brought in receipts of £8,872 for Derby. If there was a lesson to be learned from a 6–2 victory, it was that they relaxed, lost concentration and as a consequence allowed their opponents, who until that point had been totally outplayed, to score twice – against better opposition, they could have been punished even more.

First round, second leg
29 September 1971
Dundee United 3–2 Derby County (Derby win 8–5 on aggregate)
Dundee United: McAlpine, Rolland, Cameron, Markland, Gray, Henry, Traynor, Reid, Copland, Devlin (sub W. Smith 71 mins), White
Derby County: Boulton, Daniel, Robson, Hennessey, Bailey, Gemmill, McGovern, Wignall, Butlin, Walker, Hinton
Referee: Mr E. Thomson (Edinburgh)
Attendance: 5,205

Thirty-five fans from the Sportsman's Club at the Baseball Ground would take the two-and-a-half-hour flight from East Midlands to the RAF base at Leuchars which, as the nearest airfield to Dundee, was being opened up specially for their DC3 plane to land. The flight was delayed as long as possible so that the round trip could be completed within the regulation 12 hours for the flight crew. The cost of the return trip was £15 and included a match seat ticket and a meal at the Angus Hotel where Chairman Sam Longson bought everyone a drink.

Derby were still unbeaten in the league and were in third place behind Sheffield United and Manchester United by a single point. Dundee United, meanwhile, were bottom of the Scottish First Division with just one draw from their four league games.

Derby made five changes from the team that lost against Leeds United in a League Cup replay just two days earlier with Peter Daniel, Tony Bailey, Barry Butlin, Jim Walker and Terry Hennessey all coming into the team replacing Webster, McFarland, Todd, O'Hare and Hector respectively. These changes were also with an eye on the difficult game at Newcastle United coming up the following weekend. On the morning of the game, Brian Clough told the local Dundee newspapers, 'we have a load of injuries, but we have come here to win. We don't like losing at Derby.'

Dundee United were also hit by injuries that left the match resembling a part first team, part reserve team on both sides. McFarland travelled with the team and was named a substitute but had no intention of playing unless things were going badly wrong.

The change in team meant that Hinton could play a withdrawn role in midfield allowing him to spray passes left and right. Derby took the lead on the night after just four minutes when Gemmill rolled a free kick to Hinton who hit an unstoppable shot from 20 yards into the far corner of the net.

Inevitably Hinton would turn provider with the Dundee defence playing very square and unsure across the back line. A perfect through-ball found Butlin who was able to turn swiftly and place the ball into the corner of the net past McAlpine as he rushed out. Butlin then had another shot saved by McAlpine and Hinton was shooting from long range as Derby dominated the early stages. As in the first leg, with such a huge aggregate lead Derby relaxed and were punished again.

Traynor was causing some problems from his wide position and created two good opportunities for firstly Devlin and then Copland. However, neither were able to take advantage of the situation. Some of the problems were due to Terry Hennessey who had had to fly up to Dundee on the VIP supporters' flight earlier in the day. He had just recovered from a bought of 'flu and had done very little training since the first leg some two weeks earlier. The defensive issues were not helped as Tony Bailey was playing his first game in the first team and his inexperience was showing at times. With these defensive frailties it was only a matter of time before Dundee got a reward and on forty minutes a high swinging cross came over from Sandy White for Copland to help the ball past Boulton.

With the aerial bombardment of crosses it must have been tempting to introduce McFarland to steady the ship. Copland then wasted three good opportunities to get an equaliser. They did level the scores on fifty-five minutes when the danger man Traynor hit over yet another cross from the left wing for Copland to head down to Devlin who shot past Boulton high into the net from a narrow angle.

The Traynor/Copland combination then put Dundee ahead for the first time on the night when Robson could only head a cross from Traynor into the path of Copland to score his second goal of the match. From that point on both sides settled for what they had – Dundee got a famous win and Derby cruised into the next round with an 8–5 aggregate win.

The change in interpretation of the rules of football had obviously not got as far as Scotland, with the new rules coming into force in England at the start of the season under the 'Clean Up' campaign. The tackle from behind and overly strong challenges were still allowed in Scottish games and Markland and Reid in particular were making full use of old-style rules.

The manager was clearly not happy afterwards, saying, 'I never want to see a Derby side lose so sloppily again,' and the players were told the same, although probably not so politely. There had been some suggestion from various parties that Derby deliberately fielded an under-strength team for the game, having made five changes. Manchester City had already been found guilty of that offence and their £1,000 participation fee in the competition was withheld. Derby's view was that to do this would have been an insult to the other competing clubs, supporters and not least the sponsor of the tournament who was also the club's own stadium sign sponsor. For the weekend trip to Newcastle (which Derby won 1–0) the five players who sat out the Dundee game all came back into the team with Gemmill being replaced by Durban.

After the first round of games, only one Scottish team remained in the competition – Airdrie – and the Irish teams were paired together guaranteeing one would reach the semi-final.

STOKE CITY

Second round, first leg
20 October 1971
Derby County 3–2 Stoke City
Derby County: Boulton, Daniel, Lewis, Hennessey
(sub Bailey 66 mins), McFarland, Todd, Wignall, Powell,
O'Hare, Hector, Hinton
Stoke City: Banks, Marsh, Pejic, Bernard, Smith, Bloor,
Mahoney, Stevenson, Greenhoff, Jump (sub Jackson 45 mins), Haselgrave
Referee: Mr N. Burtenshaw (Great Yarmouth)
Attendance: 21,487

Derby had beaten Stoke 4–0 in a league game at the Baseball Ground a month earlier and were favourites to reach the semi-finals. In the league table Derby were in fourth place with Stoke in ninth, just two points behind. Coming into the game, Derby had just lost their first league game of the season, a 1–0 defeat at Manchester United. There were several team changes from the weekend, with both full-backs replaced and the midfield of McGovern, Gemmill and Durban replaced by Hennessey, Powell and Wignall.

Steve Powell, at the age of sixteen years and thirty days, beat the record set by his father, Tommy, and became Derby's youngest ever player to play in the first team – this came after only fourteen reserve team appearances. Also making his debut in the same game was seventeen-year old left-back Alan Lewis.

the Ram

Official Newspaper of Derby County F.C.

7p

No. 9 (v. Stoke City, October 20, 1971)

WE WUZ ROBBED
(OR WUZ WE?)

ALMOST TO A MAN the Press came out with the verdict after our last home match against Spurs: Derby County were robbed.

Most critics argued that both Tottenham goals should have been ruled out. GOAL ONE, they said, was scored by Martin Chivers with Alan Gilzean in an offside position. GOAL TWO, they said, was netted by Pearce after keeper Colin Boulton had had the ball knocked out of his grasp.

WE TRUST YOU NOTICED THAT NOT ONE DERBY COUNTY CLUB OFFICIAL WENT ON RECORD WITH ANY COMMENT.

Our policy is that the referee must always be right. Manager Brian Clough has warned the players never to argue with a decision.

Obviously, during the heat of the moment, they will occasionally make protest . . . but they are discouraged to the point where they risk a club fine for doing so.

Too much hot air

Too much hot air is spilled in the Press, on the tv screens and on the radio, about alleged refereeing errors costing points.

It does the game's image no good at all, and it doesn't enhance the sporting reputation of either the men who complain, nor the clubs whom they represent.

AS A CLUB WE DEPLORE THE PREVALENCE OF THE WE WUZ ROBBED THEME. IT CANNOT CHANGE A THING WHICH HAPPENED, CANNOT REGAIN A POINT ALLEGED TO BE LOST.

We do not intend to make any comment here whether we think Tottenham's goals were valid or not. It would make no difference.

If and when we have any comment to make about what happens when Rams play on the pitch . . . WE MAKE IT IN OUR OFFICIAL REPORTS TO THE FOOTBALL LEAGUE.

'We can win' says Tony

STOKE CITY were hammered 4-0 when they visited the Baseball Ground for a League game last month, so how do they view tonight's task in the Texaco Cup?

'It's a matter of us trying to do as well as we can,' says Manager Tony Waddington. 'Certainly, we have to improve on that showing.

'Apart from Manchester United, who played brilliantly—or rather, were allowed to do so—when I saw them at West Bromwich, Derby are far and away the best side I have seen this season.

'We are under a lot of pressure tonight, and not just to give ourselves a chance in the second leg on November 3. Four matches in eight days, including the League Cup replay against Oxford on Monday, is a big task for any side,' he adds.

'I see that Brian Clough has said he would think twice about going to Ireland if the draw worked out that way, and I respect his views. Personally, I don't think the Irish clubs add half as much excitement to the competition as the Scots, and I wouldn't mind a couple of Continental teams being invited to enter in future seasons,' Mr. Waddington says.

POWELL AND LEWIS FACE STOKE

Steve Powell, last season's England Schoolboy's captain, makes his first-team debut for Derby County in tonight's Texaco Cup-tie against Stoke City—just 4 weeks after his sixteenth birthday.

At 16 years and 30 days, he will be the youngest player to represent the Rams at senior level for many years, and he is joined by 17-year-old Alan Lewis.

Powell wears the No. 8 shirt, with Frank Wignall also coming into the forward line. Lewis is at left-back in place of John

Robson, and Peter Daniel plays right-back, with Ron Webster not quite 100 per cent after injury.

John McGovern, Archie Gemmill and Alan Durban are also excluded, but, says Manager Brian Clough: 'It is not a question of anybody being dropped because of poor form. A run of 18 League matches without defeat before last Saturday shows that nobody can have been playing that badly.

'Powell and Lewis deserve a chance because of their displays with the reserves, but nobody should look to them for match-winning

performances just yet.

Team: Boulton; Daniel, Lewis; Hennessey, McFarland, Todd; Wignall, Powell, O'Hare, Hector, Hinton. Subs: Mosley, Bailey.

Stoke, who beat Oxford 2-0 on Monday night to qualify for a 4th-round League Cup trip to Old Trafford next week, have returned 2,000 stand tickets, and these are on sale today from the Ticket Office in Shaftesbury Crescent. Mr. Len Shipman, President of the Football League, has been appointed official observer at tonight's game, by the International Football League Board.

RAM PIN-UP
'The King'
KEVIN HECTOR

Programme for the home leg against Stoke City.

McFarland was not known for his shooting ability from distance, but after just five minutes, Hennessey rolled a short free kick to him, he took the ball forwards and unleashed a shot from 25 yards that the England goalkeeper Gordon Banks had to tip over the bar. It wasn't long afterwards that Derby took the lead when a move started with Daniel who knocked the ball downfield for O'Hare to chase. As Banks rushed out, O'Hare took the ball past him and from a wide position on the right clipped the ball into the unguarded net.

O'Hare scored his second goal of the night eight minutes from the interval. Young Lewis was fouled by Haselgrave and Hinton's free kick was hit beyond the far post where Wignall headed powerfully back across goal. Banks could not hold the header and it fell nicely for O'Hare to score. Kevin Hector, who had made little impression on the game, added a third ten minutes into the second half when his left-foot shot caught Banks off his goal line and with the score at 3–0, Derby should have been safely into the semi-finals of the competition.

The game was turned on its head shortly afterwards when Hennessey, who was commanding the midfield area with his experience and strength along with Powell's calm passing, was carried off with a twisted knee when he tried to challenge a Stoke player. Tony Bailey came on to replace him at centre-half, with Todd moving into the vacant midfield role. Although no fault of Bailey's, this incident threw Derby out of their stride and Stoke dominated the last twenty minutes. Derby's attacks were reduced to the odd breakaway which produced little in the way of shots on goal.

Less than five minutes after the Hennessey injury Stoke had reduced the arrears through a simple goal. Haselgrave pushed the ball out wide to full-back John Marsh who sent over a routine cross that was met by Mahoney running in from midfield and he planted a header into the top corner.

As the game moved into injury time a Haselgrave corner was headed in at the near post by Denis Smith with the Derby defenders looking at each other questioning the marking. The conditions deteriorated during the game with the pitch becoming very heavy; Stoke came back strongly and kept the tie alive and the second leg on 3 November would be worth watching.

Both Powell and Lewis made competent debuts with Powell the most noticeable as he was heavily involved in the midfield area, particularly during the first half. Lewis grew in confidence as the game went on and put in a very creditable performance.

Second round, second leg
3 November 1971
Stoke City 1–1 Derby County (Derby win 4–3 on aggregate)
Stoke City: Banks, Marsh, Pejic, Bernard, Smith, Bloor, Haselgrave, Mahoney, Conroy, Eastham (sub Stevenson 62 mins), Jump
Derby County: Boulton, Webster, Robson, Todd, Hennessey, McGovern, Durban, Wignall, O'Hare, Hector, Hinton
Referee: Mr J. Hunting (Leicester)
Attendance: 23,461

Stoke's recent results in the league and cup were impressive with just one defeat in their previous seven games, which included a 2–0 win over Tottenham Hotspur and a League Cup victory over Manchester United. Derby had won both of their matches since the first leg, a 2–1 win at home against Arsenal and a 2–0 win at Nottingham Forest in which McFarland sustained a back injury that would keep him out for two games.

With Stoke having to force the pace of the game, being only a goal down from the first leg, it was inevitable that they would apply some early pressure. Having negotiated that period, the game settled down and was largely controlled by the Rams from then onwards who were mindful they could not afford any slip-ups.

The start of the match saw the usually reliable Todd underhit a back pass in only the second minute, releasing Conroy down the right, but he was unable to take advantage of this and pulled a tame shot past the post. After this initial frantic start by the home team, the game settled down and Derby's superior and controlled passing gradually dominated the play and pushed the Stoke midfield and defenders further and further back up the field. Stoke's deployment of the offside trap caught Derby out time and again, in particular Hector, as they continually probed for a way through. Shots began to be fired at Gordon Banks, firstly from McGovern then two from Robson before Derby's best chance came from the unlikely source of Ron Webster. Hector got past Marsh on the left and crossed into the penalty area where Webster arrived late and unmarked, his diving header going a couple of yards past the post.

Derby took the lead with a lucky but, overall, deserved goal on fifty-nine minutes. A Durban pass found Webster breaking into the Stoke area and he pulled the ball back to Frank Wignall. Pejic tried to tackle him at the same time as he shot with the result that the ball looped up and over Banks who had started to rush out to block the anticipated shot. That goal meant that the home team had to score three goals in the last half-hour of the game so Stoke immediately brought on Stevenson to replace Eastham, who had done little in the game. Derby now took a stranglehold on the game, being 4–2 up overall, and had two excellent opportunities to make the remaining minutes more comfortable. Firstly Hector, having eventually beaten the offside trap that had frustrated him all night, took the ball round Banks only to see Stuart Jump clear his shot off the line. The other opportunity, with nine minutes left to play, came when Durban put over a superb cross to the near post where O'Hare had lost his marker Smith and met the ball at waist height. His goal-bound effort forced a magnificent save from Banks who had to throw himself backwards to prevent the ball going over the line.

With time running out fast Stoke scored with just four minutes left to go when Dennis Smith got his second goal of the tie. He hooked the ball past Boulton from the edge of the area and the 1–1 draw gave Derby a 4–3 win on aggregate. There appeared no obvious team that could stop Derby from lifting the trophy.

NEWCASTLE UNITED

Semi-final, first leg
24 November 1971
Derby County 1–0 Newcastle United
Derby County: Boulton, Webster, Robson, Todd,
McFarland, Hennessey, McGovern, Gemmill, O'Hare,
Hector, Hinton
Newcastle United: McFaul, Craig, Clark, Nattrass,
Burton, Howard, Barrowclough, Green (sub Gibb 62 mins), Macdonald, Tudor,
Hibbitt
Referee: Mr C. Thomas (Treorchy)
Attendance: 20,021

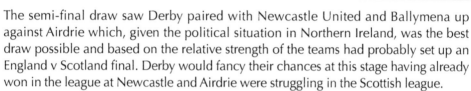

The semi-final draw saw Derby paired with Newcastle United and Ballymena up
against Airdrie which, given the political situation in Northern Ireland, was the best
draw possible and based on the relative strength of the teams had probably set up an
England v Scotland final. Derby would fancy their chances at this stage having already
won in the league at Newcastle and Airdrie were struggling in the Scottish league.

Seat tickets were the only ones sold in advance with the admission prices ranging
from £1 in the B Stand and Ley Centre down to 30p for all terracing places. The
match was televised by ITV and this triggered a further £600 payment from Texaco
as part of the ongoing sponsorship deal. Originally, Todd and Robson had been
called up to play for the England under-23 team against Switzerland at Ipswich's
Portman Road on the same night as the semi-final. Brian Clough wrote to the Football
Association stating that he wished to play his strongest possible team and permission
for the two players was duly given. The clash of fixtures had raised issues of the 'club
v country' debate with Derby firmly favouring putting the interests of the club before
anything else, as it was Derby's own supporters who were paying the players' wages.
With various meaningless international fixtures crowding the football calendar, the
opportunity to include Texaco Cup fixtures was limited.

The conditions that the match was played in were terrible; the pitch was frozen
which probably favoured the Newcastle players more than Derby. Derby's passing
game was not suited to the elements with players losing their footing regularly and
they were finding it difficult to control the ball; as for Newcastle, they had adopted a
more direct approach.

Unfortunately for the fans present, there was just one goal to show – John O'Hare
picked up a Gemmill pass, turned and curled the ball into the corner of the net.
Seconds after the goal, Newcastle forced Boulton to block a shot from Hibbitt and
another from Barrowclough. With players skidding in all directions, McFarland was
booked for a body-check on Barrowclough, with the referee making little allowance
for the conditions underfoot.

Kevin Hector had a very good chance to make the game safe following a long
corner that cleared everybody and landed at his feet, only for him to shoot over the
top. O'Hare seemed to be the one player whose balance and skill was not diminished
by the conditions and with instructions from the manager to get players into the

Newcastle penalty area at every opportunity as mistakes would happen, O'Hare set up decent chances for Gemmill (well saved by goalkeeper McFaul) and McGovern, whose shot cleared the bar. Terry Hennessey connected onto Gemmill's pass and hit a stunning low shot from 25 yards which beat the goalkeeper but went agonisingly wide and an O'Hare header was cleared off the line by Burton.

Tony Green, the Scottish international and big-money buy from Blackpool, was starting to have more and more influence on the game and began to dominate the midfield area. Unfortunately for Newcastle he had to go off after sixty-two minutes and after that they were never as dangerous. The last goalscoring opportunity came four minutes from the end when Robson put Hector through who did everything right by placing the ball beyond McFaul's left hand – it looked destined for the net, but then hit a divot a yard from goal that sent it wide.

Given the difficult conditions, Derby were happy with a 1–0 victory but recognised that with such a slender lead the return match left no margin for error. After the game the Newcastle manager, Joe Harvey, said he was also 'quite satisfied' with the scoreline, realising that there were still ninety minutes to play and plenty of opportunity to overturn the result. Newcastle had won the Fairs Cup in 1969 and were familiar with the European format of two-legged matches and how to approach them. Harvey said, 'It's wide open, a situation in which our Fairs Cup experience could stand us in good stead. Pitch conditions were better than I expected and allowed a fair game of football.' In the second leg, they would hope that Malcolm Macdonald would continue his fine form and create opportunities for others, as he was a constant threat during the first game.

In the other tie, Airdrie had won 3–0 against Ballymena. Due to the political unrest in Northern Ireland, this 'home' game for Ballymena was played at Stranraer which was the closest point to Northern Ireland where the game could be played.

Semi-final, second leg
8 December 1971
Newcastle United 2–2 Derby County (Derby win 3–2 on aggregate)
Newcastle United: McFaul, Craig, Clark, Nattrass, Burton, Howard, Barrowclough, Green, Macdonald, Hibbitt, Coulson (sub Gibb 68 mins)
Derby County: Boulton, Todd, Webster, Hennessey, Bailey, Daniel, Durban, McGovern, O'Hare, Hector, Hinton (sub Walker 68 mins)
Referee: Mr F.M. Nicholson (Manchester)
Attendance: 37,140

Derby were going to have to play the game without McFarland, Gemmill and Robson, knowing that defending such a slender lead without those players would be a struggle in front of a noisy and passionate St James' Park crowd. Todd moved to right-back, with Webster changing to the left, Hennessey and Bailey came in as central defenders, and Daniel played in midfield. This was going to be Tony Bailey's hardest game to play in since he joined the club from Burton Albion, especially as within the first minute he found himself in referee Nicholson's notebook for a foul on Macdonald. Bailey could count himself unlucky as there were other incidents in the first few minutes involving other players who also deserved to be cautioned.

For the first quarter of an hour Derby had pinned Newcastle in their own half as they tried to increase on the lead gained from the first leg but never really had a good shot on target. During those early stages it became obvious that Hinton was not going to be having one his better games and Hector lacked his usual sharpness but at least O'Hare was winning everything and was the focal point of all attacking moves.

Macdonald was proving a handful for Bailey and had one shot go across the goal while another went into the net before the linesman ruled it out for offside. The increasing Newcastle pressure was finally rewarded on the stroke of half time when Macdonald was on the end of a through-ball with the Derby defence again looking for offside and he beat Boulton with ease to level the aggregate scores.

After an hour, Newcastle took an overall lead for the first time when the influential Green gave Barrowclough a clear shot at goal which he duly scored from. With a little over twenty minutes to go and Newcastle ahead in the tie, both teams made a substitution – Jim Walker replacing the ineffective Hinton for Derby and Gibb replacing the debutant Coulson for Newcastle. It was the Derby substitute who had an immediate impact when Walker scored after seventy-three minutes, more by luck than by judgment. Hector's shot had been blocked and Durban chased the ball as it ran away from the goal. He managed to get a centre back into a crowded penalty box and an attempted clearance hit Walker and rebounded past the helpless McFaul.

With the aggregate scores now level, Derby became more dominant and Newcastle visibly wilted – only Macdonald posed any remaining threat and only a Webster goal-line clearance in the last minute stopped him scoring again.

With a 2–2 aggregate score, extra time was needed; Derby largely controlled it as Newcastle were now physically and mentally beaten. Three minutes from the end of the first half of extra time, McGovern sent over an inswinging corner from the left which flew straight into the net. Then, three minutes into the second period of extra time Derby took the lead on the night when Todd had time to control a centre and slam his shot past McFaul. This was the cue for the

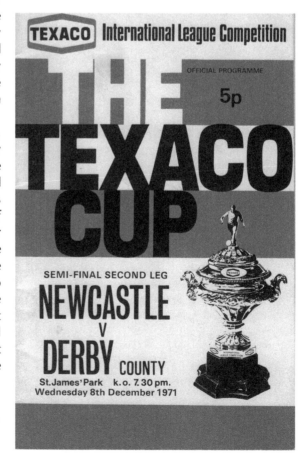

Programme for the away tie at Newcastle United.

Geordie fans to make their way home and Derby knew they had the tie won; the remaining ten minutes were played at the pace of a practice match.

The second leg attracted a huge crowd of 37,140 to Tyneside, establishing a new attendance record for the competition, beating the 30,000 who had watched Motherwell play Tottenham Hotspur in the competition a year previously.

AIRDRIEONIANS

Final, first leg
26 January 1972
Airdrieonians 0–0 Derby County
Airdrieonians: McKenzie, Jonquin, Clarke, Menzies,
McKinlay, D. Whiteford, Wilson, Walker, Busby, Jarvie,
Cowan (sub J. Whiteford 71 mins)
Derby County: Boulton, Webster, Robson, Todd, Daniel,
Hennessey, Parry, Gemmill, Butlin, Walker, Hinton
Referee: Mr W. Anderson (East Kilbride)
Attendance: 16,000

Airdrie had no major problems in their semi-final as they beat Irish team Ballymena 7–3 on aggregate. In previous rounds they had knocked out Manchester City and Huddersfield Town, both of the English First Division. Their league form, however, was poor, having taken only one point from the previous seven games and they had the worst defensive record in the division. Derby's form, in contrast, was good – winning four of the previous six games and drawing and losing one each, the most recent result being a 3–3 draw away at West Ham United.

Due to the distance involved, the club decided to fly up to Scotland for the first leg and offered places to supporters to fill up the remaining eighty-five places on the plane to join the twenty-five players and other officials that made up the official party. The return air fare was £14 which included a coach to Birmingham airport, flight to Abbotsinch airport, a meal at a hotel in Glasgow before the game and a seat ticket at Broomfield Park.

Not surprisingly, all the flight tickets sold out quickly and it was not possible to arrange a second aircraft or the 'Ramaway' train. All of Derby's allocation of seats sold out. The directions in the Derby programme before the game told those travelling by car that it is 'a straightforward journey, except that it's nearly 300 miles'. For the third successive away game Brian Clough chose not to be in attendance, being elsewhere on club business.

There was a lot of interest in Scotland regarding the game, with a sell-out, all-ticket crowd expected. As the Derby programme for the FA Cup match against Shrewsbury Town said, 'Forget the fact Airdrie are bottom of Division One – they are in the frame of mind to give Derby a match to remember'.

Tony Parry had been signed from Clough's former club Hartlepool United during the previous week and he was handed his debut in the game – his experience from playing in the Fourth Division and the style of football came in handy.

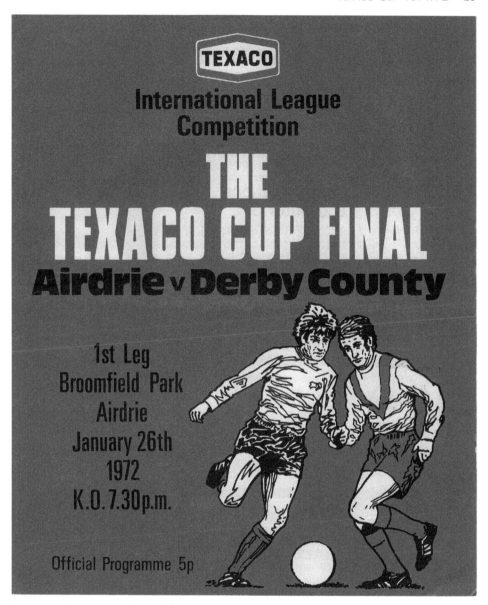

Programme for the Texaco Cup final first leg at Airdrie.

Derby were missing McFarland, O'Hare and Hector which meant that Colin Todd was given the captaincy for the first time and the replacement players – Daniel, Hennessey, Walker and Butlin – had not played for more than three weeks.

The same physical approach that they came up against when they played Dundee United in the first round was evident again with the Airdrie players getting in some rough challenges. Boulton had an early lesson when he was barged by the Airdrie forward Drew Jarvie – he soon learnt to kick the ball long, hard and quickly to avoid any further rough treatment, especially with the Scottish referee offering little protection. The Scottish team, although struggling in the league, were roared on by a partisan and, as usual for a Scotland v England encounter, ferocious crowd that meant many early tackles tended to be overzealous and required cool heads from the Derby players.

For all the tough tackles, once the initial excitement had died down Derby's defence remained firm. Despite a couple of early attempts at the Derby goal, the Airdrie forwards were kept quiet and the Scottish midfield players found it hard to create space and time to mount any serious attacks when faced with Gemmill and Hennessey. Tony Parry did not look out of place and also helped create a couple of chances when he moved forwards. One of those opportunities nearly fell to Barry Butlin who also connected with a Hinton cross and the ball was bobbling into the net before being hacked clear.

Airdrie were no match for Derby's skill and organisation and had to rely upon their enthusiasm, some rough tackling and the backing of the local fans. Archie Gemmill was Derby's star player on the night being involved all over the field and he also suffered several bad tackles. At the end of the game, Derby came away with a goalless draw and all to play for in the second leg at the Baseball Ground, remembering that Airdrie had already drawn at Manchester City and won at Huddersfield Town.

Airdrie's only other visit to the Baseball Ground was in 1927 for a specially arranged match to allow the Derby directors to watch two Scottish players – Bob McPhail and Bobby Bennie – who they were interested in signing. Airdrie won 1–0 that day and the two players were eventually transferred to Rangers and Hearts respectively. Both attended the first leg where they showed off the silver cigarette cases they, and the rest of the team, had been presented with on their visit to Derby.

Final, second leg
26 April 1972
Derby County 2–1 Airdrieonians (Derby win 2–1 on aggregate)
Derby County: Boulton, Powell, Robson, Durban, Daniel, Hennessey, McGovern, Butlin, Davies, Hector, Hinton
Airdrieonians: McKenzie, Caldwell, Clarke, Menzies, McKinley, Whiteford, Wilson, Walker, Busby, Jarvie, Cowan (sub Jonquin 78 mins)
Referee: Mr J. Taylor (Wolverhampton)
Attendance: 25,102

The original date for the second leg was 8 March but this game had to be postponed – although not before some Airdrie fans had travelled down from Glasgow in readiness for the game! The only date left to play the game was over a month later and turned out to be Derby's penultimate home game of the season.

The pre-match VIP dinner at the Midland Hotel was a much bigger event than the club had been used to with representatives from both teams in attendance as well as the Football League, Scottish League and the competition sponsors, Texaco. Derby had to pick themselves up from a 2–0 defeat at Manchester City at the weekend, a result that took City to the top of the league table in what was their last game and saw Derby slip to third position with Liverpool in second place.

Kevin Hector in action during the second leg of the Texaco Cup final.

Alan Durban receives the Texaco Cup from Len Shipman.

Derby had to make several team changes for the game with McFarland, Todd, Gemmill and O'Hare all rested as there was still a potential title-winning game to play on the following Monday night against Liverpool. Steve Powell came into Webster's right-back position for his fifth appearance in the first team with Daniel, Hennessey, Butlin and Davies filling the other places. This was Roger Davies's debut, having arrived from Worcester City for a fee of £15,000, a record transfer fee for a non-league player.

Ticket prices for this cup final were £1 for the best seats in the Ley Stand Centre and B Stand and a terracing place on the Popside cost 30p.

One of the most respected referees in England took charge of the game – Jack Taylor from Wolverhampton who would later referee the 1974 World Cup final – and it was hoped that he would be applying the rules as played in England. Unfortunately for the game, however, he let many bad challenges from the Airdrie players go unpunished and the Derby players were fouled as soon as they dwelt on the ball for any period of time. This made for a poor game to watch with the constant stop/ starting. Only one Airdrie player was booked, the centre-half Columb McKinley, but many worse challenges went unpunished.

Although, as in the first game, Derby dominated the play, it was difficult for them find a consistent rhythm because of the constant stopping for fouls and the fact that they were playing with half of the reserve team. Butlin, Davies and Hector all had good attempts at goal saved and it wasn't until the fortieth minute that Derby broke the deadlock. McKenzie, the goalkeeper, fumbled a cross and as Hector was about to pounce, he was pulled down allowing Hinton to smack the resulting penalty kick in just under the bar.

Derby doubled their lead just six minutes into the second half after squandering a few earlier chances. Butlin was the provider as he skipped a tackle on the right and crossed from the corner flag area, picking out Davies who planted a header in at the near post. More Derby chances came along as the one-way traffic continued, which included Hector hitting a post. As Derby poured forward they left gaps at the back and Airdrie exploited one of these with twelve minutes to play when Whiteford slotted home, making for a nervous last few minutes.

Colin Boulton continued to suffer at the hands of the Airdrie forwards with their late and physical challenges. Eventually he lost his temper and punched Jarvie, receiving a lecture from referee Taylor (he was later fined by Brian Clough for his behaviour).

Alan Durban, captain for the night, received the trophy from Len Shipman, president of the Football League (the actual trophy has not been seen since the final trophy match in 1975 when Newcastle United beat Southampton 3–1). Overall the club made a profit in the competition of £40,000, had attendances of over 20,000 in all of their four home games, won the trophy and had gained some valuable experience in the home and away format that would stand them in good stead in the following season's European Cup.

Derby had used twenty-two players during the competiton, a mixture of first team and reserves, with only Hennessey, Boulton and Hinton playing in all eight matches. Each player playing in the final received a bonus of £30 plus an additional £100 for winning the trophy.

Derby had lifted the Texaco Cup but within a week they had added the Central League title and, shortly afterwards, the League Championship.

TEXACO CUP 1971/72

First Round

15 September 1971	Derby County 6–2 Dundee United	
19 September 1971	Dundee United 3–2 Derby County	(W 8–5 on agg)

Second round

20 October 1971	Derby County 3–2 Stoke City	
3 November 1971	Stoke City 1–1 Derby County	(W 4–3 on agg)

Semi-final

24 November 1971	Derby County 1–0 Newcastle United	
8 December 1971	Newcastle United 2–2 Derby County	(W 3–2 on agg)

Final

26 January 1972	Airdrieonians 0–0 Derby	
26 April 1972	Derby 2–1 Airdrieonians	(W 2–1 on agg)

European Cup 1972/73

Top Ten Division One, 1971/72

Team	P	W	D	L	F	A	W	D	L	F	A	Pts
Derby County	42	16	4	1	43	10	8	6	7	26	23	58
Leeds United	42	17	4	0	54	10	7	5	9	19	21	57
Liverpool	42	17	3	1	48	16	7	6	8	16	14	57
Manchester City	42	16	3	2	48	15	7	8	6	29	30	57
Arsenal	42	15	2	4	36	13	7	6	8	22	27	52
Tottenham Hotspur	42	16	3	2	45	13	3	10	8	18	29	51
Chelsea	42	12	7	2	41	20	6	5	10	17	29	48
Manchester United	42	13	2	6	39	26	6	8	7	30	35	48
Wolverhampton Wanderers	42	10	7	4	35	23	8	4	9	30	34	47
Sheffield United	42	10	8	3	39	26	7	4	10	22	34	46

As champions of the Football League, Derby took their place in the European Cup for the first time in their history. In his programme notes for the pre-season friendly against FC Den Haag at the beginning of August Brian Clough wrote, 'one great English team after another in the past ten years has failed to pass the test facing us now' – there had been only one English winner (Manchester United) and only five had ever reached the semi-finals.

Plans were already in place to replace the floodlights, but qualification for Europe meant these were brought forward with some urgency. The new floodlights were installed in each corner of the ground at a cost of £30,000, replacing those which had been crudely built on top of the Normanton and Osmaston Stands in the 1950s. This was introduced as the use of colour television across Europe increased and to support it the pitch illumination had to be twice as bright as that demanded by the old black and white system.

The draw for the first round was made in Zurich and as soon as the draw finished the respective clubs exchanged information on hotel accommodation, food, match tickets, training facilities and all the relevant details for travelling supporters.

ŽELJEZNIČAR SARAJEVO

First round, first leg
13 September 1972
Derby County 2–0 Željezničar Sarajevo
Derby County: Boulton, Powell, Daniel, Hennessey,
McFarland, Todd, McGovern, Gemmill, O'Hare,
Hector, Hinton
Željezničar Sarajevo: Janjus, D. Kojovic, Becirspahic,
Deraković, Katalinski, Bratić, Jelusic, Janković
(sub S. Kojovic 45 mins), Bukal, Sprećo, Radović (sub Saracevic 45 mins)
Referee: Mr Anton Buchell (Switzerland)
Attendance: 27,350

Derby had an indifferent start to the season as champions, with two wins, two draws and four defeats in their first eight league games which left them in sixteenth place in the table and on a run of three defeats in the last four league games. Željezničar were also not impressing in the Yugoslavian league. According to the Yugoslavian press, Željezničar would have preferred to have been drawn against anyone else other than an English team and they would have known very little about the Derby squad. Their manager watched Derby's 2–1 home defeat to Chelsea on 19 August and the poor performance would not have fooled him. As part of the same visit they were also shown various practice grounds, beauty spots and hotels.

His team were not packed with star players, their success was achieved by a high standard of teamwork and were known to be one of the fittest teams in Eastern Europe. It was a young squad of players and the coach, Milan Ribar, only made changes to it due to injury or suspension. Although they did not know much about Derby or its squad, the feeling from within the Željezničar camp was summed up by their star player and regular Yugoslav national centre forward, Josip Bukal, when he said, 'we couldn't get it tougher than drawing English opponents. To be [the] best in England means you have to be an excellent team.' They were obviously worried and the Yugoslav press were saying that they would have to play better than they ever had before to reach the second round.

The opponents flew into the country on the Sunday night prior to the game, were based at the Newton Park Hotel at Newton Solney and would return home on the following Thursday morning. On Tuesday evening a pre-match banquet was held at Ristorante la Gondola on Osmaston Road where the visiting directors were presented with a specially commissioned silver ram. That evening, the Yugoslav players would have their opportunity to train on the Baseball Ground pitch.

Although televised by the BBC for highlights (for which they paid £4,500), the Yugoslav Football Association would not allow for the game to be shown back home. As well as attracting the BBC, many of the heavyweights of the national football press were present – Brian Glanville (*Sunday Times*), Reg Drury (*News of the World*), Alan Williams (*Daily Express*) and Jeff Farmer (*Daily Mail*).

In England, referees brought in new strict rules on tackling that were not the same in Europe; tackling from behind, deliberate trips and shirt-pulling were still the norm and it all came as a bit of a shock during the first leg. Željezničar came to defend from the start and their forwards never really threatened Derby's goal. At the other end, goalkeeper Janjus was struggling to cope with the stream of Hinton corners, crosses and free kicks.

There were good opportunities for Gemmill who shot narrowly wide, O'Hare who had a header turned round the post for a corner and Hennessey whose header was cleared off the line. Hector had three openings (one when he redirected a Hennessey shot back towards goal) and the defenders were unable to keep him under control – Sprećo was the first one to be booked following a tackle from behind.

Hennessey scraped a post when a header on target would have scored and he also had three other headers and two shots all in the first half-hour when Derby totally dominated; the corner tally at that point was 15–1.

McFarland had come close to scoring on several occasions and he had the honour of scoring Derby's first ever European goal on thirty-eight minutes, a strike that he later described as a 'once-in-a-lifetime-goal'. In actual fact the slow motion television replays showed that Sprećo handled the header as it was going in. As Derby began to make claims for a penalty kick, the ball spun back over the line before a defender cleared. Both the linesman and referee gave the goal.

Having been totally outplayed in the first half, Željezničar made two substitutions at half time, but these made little difference. Five minutes into the second half, Hector crossed from the right and Gemmill's right-foot shot hit goalkeeper Janjus and the ball landed in the net. Then for the next twenty minutes Derby streamed forward and should have added to the scoreline on a number of occasions. Hector had a shot saved at the foot of a post, Gemmill had a shot blocked following a Hector through-ball and two Hennessey headers went close before the same player sent a thunderbolt shot which beat everyone only to be a fraction wide.

Bukal, one of the long-standing international players, was getting very frustrated with the whole game and was booked for retaliation after Todd had taken the ball off him.

This was the best performance of the season so far and if there was to be a criticism, it was that for near-total dominance of the game Derby only had two goals and a host of missed chances to show for it. The *Derby Evening Telegraph* summed it up by saying 'Derby County reduced Yugoslavia's champion club to tatters' and the visitors showed nothing to suggest that the second leg would be too difficult, given that Derby had a two-goal advantage and the Yugoslav defence were unable to deal with Hinton's crosses and Hector's pace.

Man of the match was Hennessey who had several attempts at goal and his tackling, passing, covering and forward runs made this his best performance in a Derby shirt. Other notable performances came from his midfield partners Gemmill and McGovern. Also effective was Peter Daniel who came into the team to replace David Nish who was ineligible to play, having been signed past the transfer deadline for European matches. John Robson was out injured.

One disappointment on this historic night was the attendance for the game which was 27,350 (generating receipts of £18,367.43), one of the lowest home attendances during the whole season.

Special glossy programme cover for Derby's first European Cup game.

First round, second leg
27 September 1972
Željezničar Sarajevo 1–2 Derby County (Derby win 4–1 on aggregate)
Željezničar Sarajevo: Janjus, D. Kojovic, Becirspahic, Bratić, Saracevic, Katalinski, Jelusic, Janković, Bukal (sub Radović 84 mins), Sprećo, Deraković (sub S. Kojovic 6 mins)
Derby County: Boulton, Daniel, Robson, Hennessey, McFarland, Todd, McGovern, Gemmill, O'Hare, Hector, Hinton
Referee: Mr E. Linemayer (Austria)
Attendance: 60,000

With Steve Powell being just sixteen years old, Derby had to obtain special permission and a licence from Bow Street Magistrates Court to allow him to travel and 'play for profit' while abroad. The team were staying at the Terme Hotel along with the press contingent while other guests and supporters (paying £35 for return flights, half board hotel and match ticket) stayed at the nearby Europa Hotel. With the kick-off at 8.30 p.m. it was decided that the party would stay at the hotel overnight after the game before returning home on flights leaving at 9.30 a.m. arriving back in Derby at 1.00 p.m. on Thursday, in preparation for the home game against Tottenham Hotspur on Saturday.

Chairman Sam Longson was a collector of teapots of all shapes and sizes and was delighted to receive a large oriental teapot as a gift from his counterpart at one of the receptions held prior to the game. It is still housed in a cabinet at Pride Park. The away leg was scheduled to be televised by ITV, but at the last moment Željezničar refused permission for the transmission, denying Derby fans at home the sight of their team playing away in Europe for the first time. ITV had negotiated a contract with the Yugoslav national television organisation and commentator Hugh Johns and a production crew had flown out with the team. In the end ITV switched their coverage to the Leeds United v MKE Ankaragücü game and Hugh Johns, having travelled all that way, said that it 'left me angry and speechless.'

The Koševo Stadium looked good from the outside but up close it was far from impressive with fans having to cross a sea of mud to get to it – several cars had been left abandoned! There was no shelter in the stadium and as it had been raining, the wooden benches (classed as seats) were sodden.

At the weekend Derby had been beaten 3–0 at bottom-of-the-table Manchester United and made two changes to that team, with Steve Powell and David Nish being replaced by Peter Daniel and John Robson. The local newspaper, *Strana*, spelt the Derby team's names in an unusual way – 'Bolton, Deniel, Robson, Henesi, Mackfarland, Tod, Mackgovern, Gemel, O'hara, Hector, Hinton'.

The pitch itself was not in a good condition and the goalmouths had been returfed the day before the game. During the warm-up before the game, the players rolled shots across the new, bumpy turf to give Boulton an idea of what would happen during match conditions. If the first leg was anything to go by, then Derby knew to expect a rough time and that they wouldn't get too much protection from the referee. It was important not to give the home support anything to cheer about, but they had no need for concern as they were to race into a two-goal lead within the first fifteen minutes, meaning the home team would have to score five goals to go through to

Programme for the away game in Sarajevo.

the next round. The first came after nine minutes when Hector got free on the left-hand side; his cross was only cleared as far as McGovern who squared the ball to Hinton who shot from the edge of the area all along the ground into the net past the helpless Janjus. Just six minutes later it was McGovern who went down the left and crossed for O'Hare who ran onto the ball without breaking stride to score with ease.

Katalinski was the first to be booked when he deliberately tripped Gemmill, not for the first time. Derby were in complete control of the game and their calm, controlled passing and ability to break forward from different areas of the field was a constant threat. The Yugoslav forwards hardly had a kick, with McFarland marking Bukal out of the game and Todd running around and tidying up everything else.

With half an hour to go, the home team managed to score when Sprećo evaded Daniel's challenge to shoot past Boulton, even though there was a suspicion of hand ball by the forward. That goal made little difference to the result and Derby still created more chances through O'Hare and Hector who was clean through and his shot was blocked by the overworked goalkeeper.

Janković was sent off four minutes from the end of the game for kicking and punching Todd from behind – in some ways it was too little too late from the referee as others deserved to have been dismissed over the two legs for the constant body-checking, hacking down from behind, thigh-high tackles, shirt-tugging and punching.

It is usual in some countries to light fires in the stands as a sign of surrender and to show that the fans had lost faith. With Derby winning comfortably this happened with scarves, newspapers and even the wooden seats being burned, all of which was deemed as a dangerous act by UEFA who subsequently levied a fine against Željezničar.

The *Derby Evening Telegraph* were full of praise for the performance, 'The Rams' display must be ranked as one of the finest an English side has ever produced away from home and it exposed the tatty cynicism of the Yugoslavian tactics.'

After the game Brian Clough took the team to the Europa Hotel in the centre of Sarajevo where 100 of the Derby fans were staying to say thank you – 'you can't ignore fans like that,' he told waiting press. The Yugoslav press were very complimentary about Derby over the two legs, having been 'slaughtered' in Derby, and overall they concluded that Derby was 'the best they had ever seen from a foreign side . . . Colin

Todd tonight was wonderful, but you won't let him play for England! And McFarland ... what a player!' This was a reference to the fact that Todd and Alan Hudson (Chelsea) were banned by England for refusing to tour with the England under 23 team.

The draw for the second round was made on 2 October in Rome with Derby allocated number 14. The draw was attended by Sam Longson, Mike Keeling, Stuart Webb and Peter Taylor and the draw would not disappoint with Benfica being the opponents. Fleet Street wrote off Derby's chances immediately after the draw, citing the pedigree and experience of their second-round opponents. They were expecting Benfica to cruise past Derby – 'easy prey for the Eagles' was one of the headlines in the sports pages – and Peter Taylor kept those newspaper cuttings and used them to help motivate the players in the run-up to the game. After the draw Brian Clough said, 'I am absolutely over the moon about this one, and so are the lads. This will pack our ground, with as many outside trying to get in.' Peter Taylor echoed those thoughts – 'this will be something special for our players.'

BENFICA

Benfica had knocked out Malmö of Sweden in the first round by a 4–2 aggregate, losing the first leg away 1–0 before a comfortable 4–1 win at home. Clough missed the weekend game against Ipswich Town by going to Portugal on a spying mission. What he saw did not frighten him and this confidence would be conveyed to the players.

Second round, first leg
25 October 1972
Derby County 3–0 Benfica
Derby County: Boulton, Robson, Daniel, Hennessey, McFarland, Todd, McGovern, Gemmill, O'Hare, Hector, Hinton
Benfica: José Henrique, Malta da Silva, Humberto, Messias, Adolfo, Jaime Graça, Nene, Toni, Baptista (sub Jordão 55 mins), Eusébio, Simoes
Referee: Mr B. Loow (Sweden)
Attendance: 38,500

Derby were still suffering in the league having won just one of the previous five games – including a 5-0 drubbing at Leeds United – and also being knocked out of the League Cup by Chelsea. The previous weekend's 3–1 defeat at Ipswich Town left them in sixteenth place after fourteen league games, which was just 3 points ahead of the bottom teams – Crystal Palace, Manchester United and Stoke City. They had suffered six successive away defeats in the league, so they were pleased that the first leg was at home.

Benfica arrived in Derby on Monday, staying at the Pennine Hotel in the centre of town and would return home on the Thursday after the game; they had also requested to train at the Baseball Ground on Tuesday and Wednesday mornings. The referee and linesmen (all from Sweden) would be staying at the Midland Hotel for their two-night stay.

There was a huge demand for tickets and to meet the interest from around Europe in this game from the press, a temporary additional press box had been created behind the dugout. The BBC were present to show highlights during the midweek *Sportsnight* programme and they had taken over a room at the Baseball Hotel to act as a makeshift studio. The TV gantry under the Ley Stand roof was also extended to allow additional commentators from France and Austria.

The match had been designated as an all-ticket affair with the best seats at £1.50 and terrace tickets 50p (Popside) or 60p (Paddock, Osmaston End and Normanton End). Benfica had sold 320 tickets for the game, returning 80 terrace tickets but selling all the seats they had been sent. Having safely negotiated the first round, the Derby management realised that the small pitch, closeness of the crowd and high stands at the Normanton and Osmaston ends meant that the Baseball Ground became a valuable asset compared to continental stadia, which were typically large with athletic tracks surrounding the playing area. Groundsman Bob Smith had been ordered by the manager to saturate the Baseball Ground pitch on the day of the game

Programme for the home game against Benfica.

Kevin Hector foiled during the first half.

to make it very heavy and no members of press were allowed access into the stadium before the game until after 5.00 p.m.

Benfica president, Senhor D. Borges Coutinho, said at the civic reception held by Mayor George Guest on the Tuesday evening that, 'We are overwhelmed by the generosity and the friendliness of everyone in your fine town . . . My club has travelled worldwide, but never have we received such gestures, such friendship.' It had been agreed in advance that the pennants exchanged before the start of the game would be reused for the return match in Lisbon.

Archie Gemmill returned to the team after missing the previous two games with a groin strain and John O'Hare returned after missing the Ipswich defeat with a bout of tonsillitis. Kevin Hector had been struggling to walk in the build-up to the game due to a back strain, but was fit to play and summed up the mood in the camp, recalling that, 'we did nothing different in our preparation and treated it as if it was a normal game.' John Robson moved from left-back to right-back to replace Ron Webster with Peter Daniel coming in at left-back. It was little known that Robson, an England under-23 player, was actually a two-footed player and converted to a left-back by Clough. Confusingly, in this game Robson still played in his usual number three shirt.

The pitch was greasy on top and soft underneath following the soaking it had received during the afternoon and it took Derby just seven minutes and forty-two seconds to score the first goal. Gemmill's fine run forced a corner on Derby's right and Hinton flighted his kick beyond everyone to the back post where Roy McFarland, having timed his run from the back of the penalty area to perfection, headed into the goal. On twenty-seven minutes another Hinton corner again was aimed at McFarland in the centre of the goal, but it glanced off his head and the ball looped and dropped beyond the penalty spot to find an unmarked Hector. As the ball dropped, Hector hit a left-foot volley that dipped into the top corner of the net with no defender able to get near it.

The Benfica goalkeeper, José Henrique, like his counterpart from Sarajevo in the first leg, found Hinton's crosses and corners unlike anything else he had come across before and was not sure how best to deal with them. Five minutes before the half-time break, things were to get even better with a simple but devastating move starting with Peter Daniel who made a long clearance downfield where Hector won it in the air and flicked it on. McGovern, running through the middle, controlled the ball and hit a fine shot into the far corner – reminiscent of his title-winning goal against Liverpool in May.

Although that was the end of the scoring and the second half was much more even, there were still further good opportunities for Derby (in particular Hector) to score again. In the first instance he was well placed for what seemed a routine header but missed, and in the second he beat two men along the goal line at the Osmaston End and tried to shoot from a near-impossible angle while there were other players in front of goal waiting for a cross.

A 3–0 advantage after the first leg would stand them in good stead for the return at the formidable Estádio da Luz in two weeks' time and a place in the last eight of the competition was within sight. George Edwards wrote that the supporters 'were paralysed by brilliance in thirty-five minutes' in a reaction to the first-half performance. Eusébio, a man of few English words, said 'Derby good, very good,' although he was less than complimentary about the state of the pitch! Benfica's sportsmanship shone through, despite the torrid time they suffered in the first half and they never resorted to any rough tactics that other European clubs may have tried.

Malcolm Allison, manager of the Manchester City team that included such household names such as Francis Lee, Colin Bell, Mike Summerbee, Joe Corrigan and Tony Book, could only muster one word at half time – 'unbelieveable.' At the end of the game he said, 'Derby were simply magic and I can't see them dropping this sort of lead to any side in the world.' David Coleman, BBC commentator, said 'this was the best all-round performance I have seen from an English side in the European Cup. And that first half was sheer vintage stuff!' The senior writer for the Portugese football paper, Bola, reported, 'It's a long time since I saw Benfica so outplayed . . . I've never seen Benfica made to look so bad.'

Roy McFarland said in his programme notes for the next issue that, 'the atmosphere was cracking with tension . . . and this team of ours thrives on the big occasion. Without doubt, I have never played in a Rams team which played such good football for 90 minutes as we did on Wednesday.' Scorer Hector, meanwhile, said, 'We played out of our skins and they never got a kick!' Jimmy Hagan, the Benfica manager, said, 'I was very disappointed with our display in the first half but we are not without hope.'

Second round, second leg
8 November 1972
Benfica 0–0 Derby County (Derby win 3–0 on aggregate)
Benfica: José Henrique, Malta da Silva, Humberto, Messias, Adolfo, Jaime Graça,
Nene (sub Jordão 58 mins), Toni, Baptista (sub Rodrigues, 63 mins), Eusébio,
Simoes
Derby County: Boulton, Webster, Robson, Hennessey, McFarland, Todd,
McGovern, Gemmill, O'Hare, Hector, Hinton
Referee: Mr R. Schaeur (Belgium)
Attendance: 75,000

Benfica were virtually invincible on their home ground, losing only one of their thirty league games the previous season and conceding only sixteen goals while scoring eighty-one themselves – these statistics makes the 3–0 victory from the first leg seem even better!

The official party left the Baseball Ground at 9.30 a.m. on Monday and was scheduled to arrive back at 1.00 p.m. on Thursday. For the supporters it included the chance to play golf at the Estoril course and a sightseeing tour of Lisbon. There were 600 tickets available for Derby fans at a price of £3 each, all travelling on three flights from East Midlands airport.

Roy McFarland summed up the thoughts of everyone from Derby, 'Benfica are one of Europe's top sides, one of the favourites for the trophy and they won't be pushed out without a fight.' Defensively McFarland and Todd in particular would have to be at their very best and should the team have any opportunities to counter-attack, then these would be taken full advantage of. At the weekend Derby suffered a heavy defeat, 4–0 at Manchester City, and their away record so far in the season was disastrous. O'Hare and Hector both missed that Maine Road defeat and Hinton was injured during the game. The Rams had lost seven out of the previous eight away games, the only win being in the away leg of the previous round.

Unfortunately for Benfica, Hinton was fit to start and O'Hare and Hector came back into the team. Clough decided that a more experienced head was going to be required in defence; Ron Webster, who had been left out of the previous nineteen games and didn't even travel to the Željezničar away game, replaced Steve Powell at right-back. Although the players were the same, the formation and style of play was going to be radically changed for this game. They expected an onslaught and so went into the game with a defensive attitude.

There were rumours prior to the game that the star player Eusébio was injured and would not play, but these came to nothing. Benfica, having to score at least four times, realised that time was not on their side so were quick to take every throw, goal kick and free kick. The pressure on the Derby goal was constant and during this early spell they were forced to give away too many corners for comfort. Fortunately when the corner kicks were taken they usually found the head of McFarland or Hennessey and there followed a punt downfield to try to find a Derby forward to hold the ball up for a brief time to relieve the pressure.

Three times in the first twenty minutes Eusébio managed to get through only to be faced with Colin Boulton who came out on top on each occasion, blocking the shot or grabbing the ball. Even the floodlights failing (or being deliberately switched off)

Official Benfica newspaper for the game.

during one of these attacks could not beat the Derby keeper. Benfica were becoming frustrated as they didn't usually meet such a defence during their domestic matches – McFarland and Todd were at their best and backed up the experience of Webster and Robson, once he had got the measure of the winger Nene. With Boulton behind them and Hennessey playing just in front, it was a formidable back line.

Derby's best chance of the night came on sixty-three minutes. Robson passed to Hector who beat his marker Messias and then flicked the ball past the goalkeeper, José Henrique, who had rushed out of his area. However, as he was about to tap the ball into the open goal, Hector was crudely brought down by the goalkeeper and needed lengthy treatment. A clear sending-off offence, Henrique wasn't even booked and instead of being 1–0 up Derby had a free kick.

As time ticked by the 75,000 people, mainly Benfica fans, became quieter as they realised they would not be progressing to the quarter-finals of the competition this season. Roy McFarland praised the contribution of Terry Hennessey saying that he probably played the best game of his short Derby career by sitting in front of the back four, breaking up the Benfica attack before they got too close, making the defence's job that much easier in the face of fierce pressure. It was only a pity that the majority of Derby fans were unable to see his performance.

Brian Clough said, 'Even if we'd been issued with those Belgian sub-machine guns, that they give to NATO, we couldn't have stopped them. There just seemed to be waves of red shirts.'

It is a measure of Derby's aggregate victory over Benfica that in this 1972/73 season, Benfica became the only club in Portugal to go through a whole season without a league defeat. As part of that run they won twenty-eight matches (out of thirty), including a remarkable twenty-three consecutive wins. Also, Eusébio became Europe's top scorer with forty goals and the team as a whole scored 101. Derby County became only the second club (Ajax being the other) in European football history to be able to keep a clean sheet against Benfica over the two legs.

Having found some formula to defend in this game, the Rams approached away games with a new-found confidence and only lost one of the next seven away fixtures. Having knocked out one of the leading clubs in Europe, Derby would want to avoid the two favourites for the competition – Ajax of Amsterdam and Bayern Munich – while the weakest team left in the competition was the Czechoslovakian team, Spartak Trnava. The full draw for the quarter-finals was made by the West German winger Jürgen Grabowski at the German FA headquarters in Frankfurt on 24 January 1972. Stuart Webb, along with directors Bill Rudd and Bob Innes, were in attendance to see Derby drawn against Spartak Trnava. The considered opinion from behind the Iron Curtain was that Spartak would be no match for Derby whose win against Benfica in the previous round had been noticed throughout Europe.

Following the draw, lots of money from all over Europe was being placed on the winner of the Ajax v Bayern Munich tie to lift the trophy. Derby were not out of the running, though, being third favourites and having drawn the weakest team left in the competition. Brian Clough commented on the draw by saying, 'It's only a good draw if we beat them. Even though we know damn all about this Czech side there oughtn't to be anything there to really worry us. We have the skill and we have the talent – if we get our share of the luck, we can hope to make a big impact.'

Bill Shankly, Liverpool manager, writing in the *Inside Football* paper forecast Derby not only to win the European Cup, but also the FA Cup, saying 'The team is not packed with big names but it's pretty useful.'

SPARTAK TRNAVA

Spartak were on their mid-season winter break which
finished four days before the first leg. At the halfway
point of their season they were in second place behind
Prešov. Having the winter break made it difficult for the
Derby scouts to get an advance look at the opposition as
they were only playing a handful of friendly matches. The
Zimny Stadium is located in centre of the Trnava, directly
behind the walls of the old town and in 1972 had no floodlights
so the kick-off would be brought forward to the afternoon.

Quarter-final, first leg
7 March 1973
Spartak Trnava 1–0 Derby County
Spartak Trnava: Kéketi, Dobias, Majernik, Hagara, Varadin, Hrusecky, Fandel,
Masrna, Horvath, Adamec, Kabát
Derby County: Boulton, Powell, Nish, O'Hare, McFarland, Todd, McGovern,
Gemmill, Davies, Hector, Durban
Referee: Mr Karoly Palotay (Hungary)
Attendance: 25,000

This game was the first time that Derby had to play away from home in the first leg
and the aim would be to score the all-important away goal if possible and to restrict
the home team as much as possible. The official party flew from Heathrow to Vienna
on Monday 5 March at 10.30 a.m. and they eventually arrived at the Magnolia Hotel
in Trnava at 5.00 p.m. which gives some measure of the difficulty in getting from
Vienna to Trnava. After the game the party would relocate to the Inter-Continental
Hotel in Vienna in preparation for a flight home on Thursday. Some 500 Derby fans
made the trip, some on a one-day trip costing £38, and others staying for three days
costing £43.

On Tuesday, some 1,500 locals turned up for the Derby training session at the
stadium with the Spartak chairman explaining that English football is held in high
regard in Czechoslovakia and the locals were keen to see the training methods used
and to get an early glimpse of the Derby players.

The Derby fans were faced with an eventful journey to the game – leaving their
Vienna hotel at 7.30 a.m. for the 2.30 p.m. kick-off even though it was only 50 miles
away. The journey had to include a one-hour stop at the border while everyone's
hands and shoes were cleaned thoroughly owing to a foot and mouth outbreak.

David Nish had been transferred from Leicester City for a British record fee of
£250,000 to replace John Robson who had moved down the A38 to Aston Villa for a
Derby record receipt fee of £90,000. This was the first time Nish was eligible to play
in the competition. Derby had climbed to sixth place in the league but had lost four
out of the previous six games including a 3–2 home defeat to Leeds United at the
weekend. The team had a different look to it with Alan Hinton and Terry Hennessey
out injured – Roger Davies had come into the team with John O'Hare playing a more

Spartak programme from the first leg

ŠTVRŤFINÁLE PEM VO FUTBALE

SPARTAK
TRNAVA

DERBY
COUNTY

TRNAVA – 7.marca 1973 o 14,30 hod.

withdrawn role and Alan Durban coming back into the starting eleven. Clough had promised before the game that Derby had not come to do the usual defensive display of away teams, but to attack and entertain.

It was Derby who created the first chance of the game after seven minutes when Alan Durban flashed a low diagonal ball across the penalty area to the far post and John O'Hare couldn't quite make contact with the ball. For the rest of the half it was Trnava who dominated possession, albeit without forcing Colin Boulton into any difficult saves. The Trnava players were making it difficult for the Derby midfield to find any time and space and so the front players were isolated and Adamec, Horvath, Kabát, Dobias and Hagara were bringing the ball out of defence and starting all of the Trnava attacks.

The inexperience of Steve Powell was showing and he was having a difficult time against Kabát, but Colin Todd was providing cover on the right and was in superb form. Four minutes from half time, however, Trnava scored when Todd tried to play his way out from the penalty area, beating two players but then losing the ball to a third, Fandel. He played the ball through to Horvath who put a left-foot shot from just outside the penalty area into the top corner of the net with the other Derby defenders a little slow to react.

The second half was a totally different performance from Derby as they reorganised and began to dominate and push forwards, but without Hinton they couldn't find the quality of pass or cross to force an equaliser. The tackling from the Czech side became more desperate as the game went on and there were some rough tactics used to try to put off the Derby midfield and forwards. On fifty-seven minutes, in a similar move to the one in the first half, Hector drove over a cross only for Roger Davies to fail to convert the opportunity. Shortly afterwards, Derby had the ball in the net when Durban's through-ball split the defence and allowed Davies a run on goal – he duly put the ball into the net, only to turn around to see a linesman flagging him as offside. This decision was hotly disputed and the Derby fans, who were in line with the incident, suggested that he was onside when the ball was played.

Another golden chance came on seventy-five minutes when an excellent build-up and passing combination between Durban and O'Hare released John McGovern

Spartak fans with their banner.

who attempted to slide the ball into the far corner from close range but he scuffed the ball allowing the goalkeeper Kéketi to make the save.

Dobias was eventually booked for his continued assault on Hector and the referee was very lenient – it would not have been a surprise to see the player sent off for his continual fouling. Following another foul that was considered to be a second bookable offence that went unpunished, McFarland questioned the referee and found himself in his notebook, an incident he would later regret. Derby deserved something from the game on the balance of play – a draw at the very least.

Trnava's only other clear chance came a few minutes before the end of the game when David Nish slipped and allowed Masrna a clear run from the halfway line. Colin Boulton raced from his goal to the edge of the penalty area, waited until the forward made the first move, then blocked the shot with his legs to preserve the scoreline. Generally the home side were restricted to long-range and wayward efforts.

Derby were happy enough with a 1–0 defeat – their first in Europe – and were confident that the result could be overturned in the return match a fortnight later. There were fine performances throughout the team with Colin Todd being the star player despite being responsible for the only goal. Todd was still under a two-year ban from the England team following refusal (along with Alan Hudson) to tour with the England under-23 team – on this form it was England who were the ones to suffer.

Anton Malatinsky, the Spartak manager, said, 'I don't think we've done quite enough. I wish we could have got at least two goals today.' A lack of phone lines from the stadium meant that just three journalists – Barrie Eccleston of Radio Derby, Peter Jones of BBC Radio and Frank Clough of the *Sun* – were the only ones to get any sort of connection back to the UK; everyone else had to wait until they got back to Vienna to file their report. The travelling media's general opinion was that the tie was very much in Derby's control but they would have to get past what would surely be a stiff East European-style defence. It would be a major surprise, however, if Derby could not turn around the one-goal deficit in the second leg.

Despite the feeling of Czechoslovakia being a bit downtrodden, the hospitality (of the town and football club) made it a memorable trip for all concerned, although one of the Derby directors said, 'I'll be glad to get home to toast and two boiled eggs.' Roy McFarland commented that the country was, 'very drab . . . even the countryside was flat and grey . . . but the Czechs are a great and friendly people.'

Quarter-final, second leg
21 March 1972
Derby County 2–0 Spartak Trnava (Derby win 2–1 on aggregate)
Derby County: Boulton, Webster, Nish, O'Hare, McFarland, Todd, McGovern, Gemmill, Davies, Hector, Hinton
Spartak Trnava: Kéketi; Dobias, Majernik, Hagara, Kuna, Hrusecky, Horvath (sub Varadin 58 mins), Masrna (sub Martinkovic 7 mins), Fandel, Adamec, Kabát
Referee: Mr Angonese (Italy)
Attendance: 36,472

Not surprisingly the match was an all-ticket game with the best seats in the B Stand costing £1.75 and terrace tickets were 60p, an increase on the previous rounds. ITV would be covering the game for a fee of £6,000 with the potential of additional sales to other countries at £500 per country.

Derby knew exactly what they had to do to get through to the semi-finals, a minimum of a two-goal margin of victory would be needed. They would hope to get an early breakthrough and it was well known that few East European sides could survive sustained pressure, so one goal should lead to many more. However, there was no room for error with the away goals counting double in the event of an aggregate draw. Derby had been knocked out of the FA Cup at the quarter-final stage the previous weekend by Leeds United through an own goal by David Nish. This defeat was the fourth defeat in the last five games and they had failed to score in the last three.

The Spartak team arrived at Birmingham on Monday and would be based at the Riverside Hotel in Burton for three nights. They had planned to train at the Baseball Ground on Tuesday evening before a cocktail party for officials and press at the stadium.

Alan Hinton was back in the starting line-up; his groin strain had cleared up enough to get him out on the field and as was found out in first leg, he was a hugely important and influential player. Trnava were able to welcome back Kuna, who was suspended for the first leg and was thought to be as influential to their team as Hinton was to Derby. David Nish was struggling with an injury, but thought fit enough to play even though not fully 100 per cent.

OFFICIAL PROGRAMME: Cup Special

THE RAM

Price—Seven new pence   The Official Newspaper of Derby County Football Club   Vol 2, No 25, Wednesday 21st March, 1973 (v Trnava 7.30 p.m.)

WELCOME IN THREE TONGUES

WE WELCOME tonight our guests from Spartak Trnava, and it is our wish that they enjoy their stay among us as much as we did our stay with them in their country a fortnight ago.

And may the best team win through to the semi-final round of the European Cup.

In Czech translation this reads:

Je n nám potěšením uvítať dnes večer na tomto fotbalovém hřišti naše přátele ze Spartaku Trnava a věříme, že jejich pobyt v naší zemi bude stejně hezký, jako byl náš pobyt v Československu před dvěma týdny.

Ať lepší mužstvo zvítězí a postoupí do semifinále Evropského poháru.

As Spartak Trnava are a Slovak team we also give out message in the Slovak language.

Je nám potešením uvítať dnes večerna tomto futbalovom ihrisku nasích priastelov zo Spartaku Trnava a veríme, že ich pobyt v našej krajine bude taký prijemný a pekný, aký bol náš pobyt v Československu pred dvoma týždňami.

Nech lepšie mužstvo zvíťazí a postúpi do semifinále Európskeho poháru.

CASH DOUBTS IN EURO CUP

But we're sure our lads will get what they earn

Out into the Zimny Stadium at Trnava come the Derby County and Spartak Trnava teams a fortnight ago.

Chairman Mr. Sam Longson, recovering from his recent illness in a Manchester hospital, has had visits from a number of Derby County directors and officials.

He has also had surprise visits from Sir Matt Busby and Tommy Docherty, a basket of fruit from Manchester City F.C. and flowers from Manchester United.

RUMOURS that Derby County will not be allowed to pay their players win bonuses, in the event of their winning the European Cup, are premature.

The Government's new Counter-Inflation Bill soon to become law will not affect footballers bonuses, even if it does affect players' wages.

Football law prevents clubs from altering the amount of players' wages, except during the close season or when a professional reaches his 18th or 21st birthdays.

Derby's players have a special amount written into their contracts for every European Cup game they play, but there is no amount specified for their winning the trophy.

If the new Bill limits the pay increases allowed to £250 a year there will be nothing to prevent back-dated bonus clauses from being inserted into their contracts.

It is more likely, however, that professional footballers will continue to be regarded in the same light as film stars, actors etc who are paid specific sums for specific jobs done.

However the situation develops, it is most unlikely that Derby County will be prevented from paying their players for work done.

The Spartak Trnava pennant.

Programme from the home leg against Spartak.

The first period of play showed everyone watching that Spartak would not be easy to beat and they were the best team the Baseball Ground crowd had seen so far in the competition even if they were generally considered as the underdogs to lift the trophy. Kuna was seeing plenty of the ball and it was plain to see he was their star player. With his confidence spreading throughout the team, they were able to keep Derby largely quiet. Indeed, Spartak probably had the better of the play in the first half even without causing Colin Boulton to make a save.

Derby were restricted to a free kick by Hinton which went close and two other shots by O'Hare who also had the best chance when he flicked on a cross that had the keeper beaten but was too high. O'Hare was in excellent form but the early goal that was hoped for did not arrive and the longer the game went on, the more anxious the crowd and players would become.

Spartak, arguably, had the best opportunities from breakaways with Kabát inches away from touching in a cross from Hrusecky and Colin Todd had to hold Martinkovic to stop him from having a clear run on goal. On one of the rare occasions that Spartak gave the ball away, Adamec lost possession in midfield to Gemmill who passed to McGovern leaving him clear on the right-hand side. His low centre was slotted into the net by Hector to bring the aggregate scores level. Two minutes later Davies nearly doubled the lead when his fine run and shot narrowly missed.

Nish surprisingly came out for the second half after suffering an injury, as Derby searched for the second goal. It came when a Hinton cross was met by Davies who was bundled over and as everyone was waiting for the referee to give the penalty, Hector played on and volleyed his shot just under the bar from 15 yards giving the necessary two-goal advantage.

Alan Hinton was also suffering with his groin injury and he wasn't prepared to take on the defence directly as he usually would although he carried on as Derby continued to create chances through Davies, McGovern and Nish. As time ticked down the game became more nervous to watch as Spartak only needed to score one goal to go through on the away goals rule. The last few minutes were uncomfortable and there were many panicked clearances. To add to the tension Archie Gemmill got himself booked for protesting too much against a decision by the Italian referee – another silly booking that would be regretted. Thankfully Derby stayed strong and denied Spartak their away goal.

Financially, the European games were proving successful, with the overall profit on the tie being £23,575, and that was after the player bonuses of £200 each for the eighteen players in the squad and £1,500 each for Clough and Taylor. The gate receipts for the home leg totalled £34,000 and TV revenue came to £7,500.

Dave Sexton, Chelsea manager, said in the *Daily Mail,* 'I would bet on Derby to beat them [Ajax or Bayern] over two legs. Derby are a fine team and would not be overawed or overpowered by Ajax. Ajax against Derby would make a marvellous final.' However, first they were drawn against Juventus.

JUVENTUS

11 April 1973
Semi-final, first leg
Juventus 3–1 Derby County
Juventus: Zoff, Spinosi, Marchetti, Furino, Morini,
Salvadore, Causio, Cuccureddu (sub Haller
62 mins), Anastal, Capello, Altafini
Derby County: Boulton, Webster, Nish, Durban,
McFarland, Todd, McGovern, Hector, O'Hare,
Gemmill, Powell
Referee: Mr G. Schulenburg (West Germany)
Attendance: 72,000

Derby were in the middle of five successive away games and had won their most recent, 1–0 at Arsenal. That game was on 31 March, giving them a clear eleven days without a game as their scheduled opponents, Wolverhampton Wanderers, were in the FA Cup semi-final. This gave them time to get all the players fully fit and in the right frame of mind for, potentially, the biggest game of their lives.

The official party, including former Juventus player John Charles (who was acting as translator), left Derby at 3.00 p.m. on Sunday, flying from East Midlands airport to Turin, and they would return immediately after the game arriving back home at 11.00 p.m. the same day as it was an afternoon kick-off. The VIP party would be staying at the Turin Palace Hotel in the centre of Turin.

There was some unrest in the Derby camp when Brian Clough and Peter Taylor verbally clashed in front of the players. The night before the game there was to be a dinner for the journalists where Brian Clough would be the main speaker with Peter Taylor due to attend but not speak as he was not overly confident about appearing in front of the gathered press. At the appointed departure time, Clough was still playing cards and Taylor, who was ready to leave, stormed off back to his room following some choice words to Clough – who knows what effect this public disagreement had on the players before such a big game?

Derby had announced the team internally and there was a major surprise with Tony Parry included at the expense of Alan Durban. The squad, as usual, went for a pre-match walk and at some point during that the decision was reversed and Durban restored to the team. Roger Davies had a groin strain and would be replaced by John O'Hare and the influential Alan Hinton was still missing with his groin injury. As the 3.30 p.m. kick-off at the Stadio Comunale approached, the huge black and white flags carried by the Italian fans began waving, something the Derby team had not seen on their travels before.

The first twenty minutes were a bit strange for a semi-final with the home team happy to sit back and watch Derby pass the ball around at will and even Webster and Todd were finding the time and space to join in the forward play. In the twenty-seventh minute, however, Juventus took the lead out of nothing when Todd was beaten in the air on the Derby right and the lofted centre split McFarland and Nish allowing Altafini time to run between them and coolly slot past Colin Boulton. Two minutes later, though, Derby drew level when O'Hare played in Hector who beat Salvadore and Morini to fire one in past Zoff. This was the first goal scored by an English club in Italy in the European Cup. The only other chance of note in the first half fell to Marchetti whose shot from the right wing was cleared of the line by David Nish.

At half time the score was 1–1 with Derby having the luxury of an away goal and in a position to dictate the course of the second half and hopefully come away with a positive result. The defence was coping with the Italian forwards and the midfield was matching the Juventus players. After an altercation at half time between Juventus substitute Haller and Peter Taylor, the half-time team talk was disrupted and there did not seem to be a coherent message given to the players; they were not sure whether to attack or defend and ended up doing neither.

The game changed on sixty-two minutes when the German Helmut Haller was brought on to replace Cuccureddu who was injured after colliding with Todd. He immediately took a position out on the wing and this change in formation sparked Juventus into their best football of the game. After being on the field for just four minutes, Haller's influence had an effect as a Juventus move from the left went across the stationary Derby back line and eventually came to Causio who had time to turn and shoot into the corner of the net. Causio then hit a post before the thirty-four-year-old Brazilian José Altafini scored again seven minutes from the end which started the flag-waving among the jubilant Juve fans.

John O'Hare had an excellent game and was admired by members of the Italian press who were impressed with his ability to hold the ball and his control.

A 3–1 defeat was not the result Derby would have wanted but it could have been much worse and they were grateful for the Kevin Hector goal and knowledge that Alan Hinton could be fit enough to hopefully play an important part in the return leg. However, they would have to play the home game without Gemmill and McFarland because of the controversial bookings in the first leg; Gemmill had his name taken for a trip on Furino, retaliation after Furino's elbow had made deliberate contact with his face. McFarland's booking, however, was very strange. He jumped with Cuccureddu for a high ball and the two heads clashed and he was booked. As both Derby players had already been booked in the competition (in the matches against Spartak in the previous round) this meant an automatic one-match ban – they would have to sit out the return leg at the Baseball Ground. Furino would also miss the return but his prolonged kicking and fouling of Gemmill all over the field should have ended in more punishment than a booking. As the *Derby Evening Telegraph* described it, 'It looked like a put-up job.'

It was only after the game that the full drama of the goings-on behind the scenes became public knowledge. Peter Taylor originally raised alarm bells even before the kick-off when he came into the dressing room saying, 'Haller's in with the ref again. That's twice I've seen him.' At half time Haller, only named as a substitute, walked off with referee Gerhard Schulenburg instead of his team-mates so Peter Taylor followed them and got an elbow in the ribs from Haller and a large group of stewards and police stopped Taylor – and even tried to arrest him – before he managed to get to the safety of the Derby dressing room. John Charles, still highly respected by the Juventus supporters as a former player, calmed the incident down but by then Taylor had missed the half-time interval. This, together with the strange bookings for McFarland and Gemmill, caused Brian Clough to explode with rage after the game, 'No cheating

Juventus' club magazine, Hurra.

bastards will I talk to, I will not talk to any cheating bastards!' Brian Glanville from the *Sunday Times* spoke fluent Italian and was ordered by Clough to translate for the Italian press – which he duly did with a predictably hostile response.

This incident had a lasting effect on the management duo and after that game they always had someone watching the referee's room to stop any such thing happening again. An official complaint was made to UEFA about the referee's handling of the game but, after an inquiry, no apparent action was taken.

25 April 1973
Semi-final, second leg
Derby County 0–0 Juventus (Derby lose 3–1 on aggregate)
Derby County: Boulton, Webster, Nish, O'Hare, Daniel (sub Sims 71 mins),
Todd, McGovern, Powell (sub Durban 45 mins), Davies, Hector, Hinton
Juventus: Zoff, Spinosi, Marchetti, Furino, Morini, Salvadore, Causio,
Cuccureddu (sub Longobucco 67 mins), Anastasi, Capello, Altafini
Referee: M. Lobo (Portugal)
Attendance: 38,450

On 29 March a letter was received from UEFA regarding the limited press facilities
at the Baseball Ground. The usual facilities catered for thirty journalists and this had
been extended to over sixty by utilising additional space behind the dugouts, but
the letter suggested that even this number would be inadequate for the arrival of
Juventus. The example quoted on the letter was the recent Ajax v Bayern semi-final
game where over 200 press places were required.

The overall winners of the tie would go through to the final that was to be played
in Belgrade on 30 May with an 8.30 p.m. kick-off at the Crvena Zvezda stadium. A
possible replay date was also fixed for two days later at the same venue.

Derby knew exactly what they needed to do following the first leg – a 2–0 win
would be good enough on the away goals rule and a 3–1 victory would send the tie
into extra time and the possibility of a penalty shoot-out. The reputation of the Italians

Special directors' edition of the
programme.

Rams programme for the home leg.

WELCOME JUVENTUS: BENVENUTA JUVENTUS

WELCOME today to our Italian friends from Juventus of Turin.

We look forward to extending towards them the same warm friendship and generosity which they extended so freely to us on our recent visit to Italy.

At the end of tonight's game may the better side of the two go on to represent their country in the European Cup Final in Belgrade on May 30. In other words, may the better team win.

AI NOSTRI amici della Juventus porgiamo le espressioni di sincero benvenuto.

L'occasione odierna ci e'opportuna per ricambiare la generosa ospitalita' riser-vataci a Torino nelcorso del nostro soggiorno per la prima partita di semifinale.

Auguriamoci che al termine della gara di questa sera, la squadra che dovra' rappresentare la propria nazione nella finalissimo della Coppa Dei Campioni a Belgrado il 30 maggio, sia quella che avra' maggiormente meritato nel doppio confronto di semifinale.

was well known – there would be a lot of pushing, kicking and off-the-ball incidents as well as a no-nonsense defence. What Derby could not do was to allow Juventus to score an away goal as that would almost certainly put the tie beyond them.

Prior to the game Terry Hennessey was ruled out of action for the rest of season with injury, with similar major doubts about Alan Hinton. The team that drew 1–1 against West Ham United on the previous Saturday bore little resemblance to that selected for the Juventus game, with Graham Moseley in goal (just his second appearance) and Tony Parry (his seventh appearance) in the starting team. Due to the suspensions carried forward from the first leg, Peter Daniel replaced Roy McFarland in central defence for his fourth European game and O'Hare moved back to a midfield position. Roger Davies was fit and Alan Hinton was risked, although he was not fully fit; he had not played a game for over a month and did not play in his usual wide position.

Manager Clough shares a joke with Nish, Hector, McFarland, Davies and a reporter after training.

Ticket prices were increased again for this game – £3 for seats in the B Stand and Ley Stand Centre and £1 for a terrace ticket on the Popside. ITV had exclusive broadcast rights on the game being allowed to show 45 minutes after 10.30 p.m. The fee was £7,000 plus any revenue from sales throughout Europe (Italian TV would be charged £3,000 and any others £1,000). Player bonuses for reaching the final and winning had been agreed – £800 for playing and an additional £500 for winning the competition.

The game started well for the home team as within the first couple of minutes Juventus had given away a free kick, there were appeals for a penalty and Zoff was scrambling around his line to keep out a shot from the unlikely source of Ron Webster. This was followed shortly afterwards by shots from O'Hare and Hinton. The remainder of the first half passed without incident, with the Italians containing the Derby threat.

However, the tie was effectively over just after the hour mark. Firstly Spinosi tripped Kevin Hector in the area (the Italian's twenty-fifth foul of the game) giving Derby a huge opportunity to go ahead on the night. Unusually, Hinton missed the penalty kick, hitting it wide and high at the Normanton End of the ground. Had that gone in it was possible that Derby would have gone on to win the tie and go through to the final.

As time ticked by, it was becoming obvious that Derby were not going to progress. After sixty-three minutes Roger Davies finally snapped, punched Morini and was rightly sent off. Morini had been antagonistic throughout the game and there was a series of off-the-ball incidents that eventually came to a head. That cost him a club fine of £100 for being in breach of club disciplinary rules and was automatically suspended for the next three European matches. It also was also effectively the end of the contest as Derby had few ideas left to throw at the Italians.

With twenty minutes to go, Derby made their last substitution with Peter Daniel being replaced by John Sims and then Juventus staged some attacks of their own with Anastasi and Longobucco giving Colin Boulton some difficult saves to make. At the final whistle, the huge black and white flag-wielding Italian fans invaded the pitch as they celebrated reaching the final. Juventus did what Italian sides were renowned for – expert defending, cynical tackles and the ability to break away quickly on the counter-attack. This they did extremely well as for all of Derby's possession, they could not get a clear shot at goal very often. Even Hinton's crosses that had troubled every other team he had faced were being headed away by Salvadore and Morini. Only Manchester United had got further in the competition and Derby could hold their heads high after a successful first European campaign. One can only speculate on what would have happened if the first leg had not allegedly been fixed and the bookings of Gemmill and McFarland had not happened . . . a place in the final? A win and chance to defend the trophy? New signings? Clough and Taylor not leaving the club within six months?

With the home team keeping the gate receipts, the four ties in 1972/73 European Cup produced £135,000 in additional income and £38,000 in TV revenue. Francisco Marques Lobo, the Portuguese referee for the second leg, reported to his FA that an Italian agent (former referee Deso Solti) had offered him a bribe to favour Juventus – a UEFA sub-committee inquiry in Zurich didn't even bother to interview the main parties involved and took no action. Juventus proceeded to the final – another bribe? Over a year after the game, the *Sunday Times* (Brian Glanville and Keith Botsford) interviewed Lobo and printed the bribery story (known as the Lobo-Solti case) which did not go down well in Italy.

EUROPEAN CUP 1972/73

First round
13 September 1972	Derby County 2–0 Željezničar Sarajevo	
27 September 1972	Željezničar Sarajevo 1–2 Derby County	(W 4–1 on agg)

Second Round
25 October 1972	Derby County 3–0 Benfica	
8 November 1972	Benfica 0–0 Derby County	(W 3–0 on agg)

Quarter-final
7 March 1973	Spartak Trnava 1–0 Derby County	
21 March 1973	Derby County 2–0 Spartak Trnava	(W 2–1 on agg)

Semi-final
11 April 1973	Juventus 3–1 Derby County	
25 April 1973	Derby County 0–0 Juventus	(L 3–1 on agg)

UEFA Cup 1974/75

Top ten Division One, 1973/74

Team	P	W	D	L	F	A	W	D	L	F	A	Pts
Leeds United	42	12	8	1	38	18	12	6	3	28	13	62
Liverpool	42	18	2	1	34	11	4	11	6	18	20	57
Derby County	42	13	7	1	40	16	4	7	10	12	26	48
Ipswich Town	42	10	7	4	38	21	8	4	9	29	37	47
Stoke City	42	13	6	2	39	15	2	10	9	15	27	46
Burnley	42	10	9	2	29	16	6	5	10	27	37	46
Everton	42	12	7	2	29	14	4	5	12	21	34	44
Queens Park Rangers	42	8	10	3	30	17	5	7	9	26	35	43
Leicester City	42	10	7	4	35	17	3	9	9	16	24	42
Arsenal	42	9	7	5	23	16	5	7	9	26	35	42

Derby were still looking for another striker to join their squad – the pre-season matches had yielded just one goal in three games – and eventually the former England striker Francis Lee was signed from Manchester City, leaving the forwards available for selection as Lee, Hector, Davies, Hinton and Bourne.

The UEFA Cup competition had been slightly modified for this season and the draw was now zoned; so if the Rams were to get through round one and their fixtures with Servette Geneva, their next opponents would be one of Atlético Madrid, BK Copenhagen, SV Hamburg, Bohemians, Rosenborg or Hibs. The team to avoid were Atlético Madrid who were the previous year's European Cup losing finalists. The reason for the zoning was that there were quite a number of 'weaker' teams in the competition and UEFA wished to reduce the financial burden on those clubs due to excessive travelling.

Despite of their amateur status, Servette could not be taken lightly as they managed to beat Liverpool 2–1 in Geneva in the first round of the Cup Winners' Cup in 1971. Servette's European record suggested that it was away from home that they had problems, having lost ten of the thirteen away legs they had played to that date. Their president said, 'it's as tough a tie as we could have had.' Derby's league form had been poor with just one win in the seven games played so far – that being a 2–0 home win against Sheffield United nearly a month before. They had lost 3–2 at Birmingham City at the weekend and there were two team changes from that defeat at St Andrews, with the experience of Henry Newton replacing Steve Powell and Jeff Bourne coming in for Roger Davies, who was still serving a European suspension.

SERVETTE GENEVA

18 September 1974
First round, first leg
Derby County 4–1 Servette Geneva
Derby County: Boulton, Webster, Nish, Rioch,
Daniel, Todd, Newton (sub Hinton, 54 mins),
Gemmill, Bourne, Hector, Lee
Servette Geneva: de Blaireville, Schnyder,
Morgenegg, Martin, Guyot, Marchi, Pfister,
Castella (sub Sundermann 50 mins, sub Andrey 62 mins), Riner, Wegmann,
Petrovic
Referee: Antonio Riga Segura (Spain)
Attendance: 17,716

Servette had finished third in the Swiss championship (just as Derby had done in
England) and being amateurs were largely unknown to English fans and all of the
players had other day jobs. With the record of the Swiss teams in Europe, it was
expected to be an easy passage into the next round for the Rams with Dave Mackay

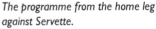

*The programme from the home leg
against Servette.*

wanting at least a three-goal lead to take into the away leg. Roy Mcfarland was out injured for the season after suffering a serious achilles injury while playing for England and Peter Daniel would take his place.

Straight from the kick-off, Petrovic hoofed the ball directly to Boulton giving the impression that they were going to be happy sitting behind the ball for ninety minutes and had little intention of venturing far into Derby's half.

It wasn't too long before Derby scored – on twelve minutes a free kick from Nish aimed towards Daniel missed everyone and Hector was on hand to head down and into the net. Lee had an effort cleared off the line before the second goal came from an unlikely source in Peter Daniel (his first goal in his 144th appearance) when he headed in a cross from Webster. Two minutes before the interval, Lee received a pass from Gemmill with his back to goal and turned, shooting past the goalkeeper. At 3–0 at the break, they were looking towards the next round as Servette were being brushed aside.

Hector scored his second goal of the night as he beat two defenders before slotting the ball past de Blaireville. Taking off Newton and replacing him with Hinton upset the balance, rhythm and flowing football that Derby were playing, and this allowed Servette back into the game as Boulton was called upon to make a couple of saves. Servette pulled a goal back when Guyot moved forward from his sweeper position and found Petrovic in space who was able to squeeze his shot past Boulton into the corner of the net.

A 4–1 win in the first leg and knowing that Derby were too strong, too fast and had too much skill, there was nothing to fear from the second leg in Geneva.

2 October 1974
First round, second leg
Servette Geneva 1–2 Derby County (Derby win 6–2 on aggregate)
Servette Geneva: de Blaireville, Schnyder, Morgenegg, Martin, Guyot, Sundermann (sub Barriquand 76 mins), Pfister, Wegmann, Riner, Andrey (sub Marchi 62 mins), Petrovic
Derby County: Boulton, Webster, Nish, Rioch, Daniel, Todd, Newton, Gemmill, Bourne, Hector, Lee
Referee: Mr Woehrer (Austria)
Attendance: 9,600

Since the first leg Derby had won two home games against Burnley and Chelsea, and had drawn at Stoke City on the Saturday before the game. There was one enforced change in the Derby team with Roger Davies again replaced by Jeff Bourne.

Servette, having to score at least three times, started strongly and they were chasing and closing down the Derby players whenever they had the ball. They had the first chance of the game in the opening minutes when a free kick from Schnyder flashed through everyone before a combination of Nish and Todd blocked the shot on the line and got the ball out for a corner. Despite the home team's strong start, Derby were able to get forward and cause problems for the shaky Swiss defence – de Blaireville saved twice from Hector before he had the ball in the net from a Rioch through-ball, but the linesman was flagging for offside.

servette
football
club

Mercredi 2 octobre 1974   -   Coupe U.E.F.A.

derby-county

servette

saison 1974/75   programme officiel fr. 1.—

Assis de gauche à droite : NISH - McGOVERN - GEMMILL - McKAY, manager - McFARLAND
HECTOR - HINTON - NEWTON.
Debout de gauche à droite : GORDON, soigneur - TODD - O'HARE - POWELL - DANIEL - BOULTON
WEBSTER - DAVIES - THOMAS - ANDERSON, manager adjoint et COACH.
Manque : LEE - RIOCH - BOURNE.

One of the two different Servette programmes from the away leg.

A shock looked possible, however, when Servette scored after nineteen minutes. Player-coach Sundermann sent over a corner which was not cleared, took a lucky rebound and fell to Martin who scored. That said, Hector almost scored immediately when his cross-shot beat the goalkeeper but bounced away off the bar and Daniel also went close following a Rioch free kick. Despite being a goal down at the interval, there did not look to be any danger of the Rams conceding any more goals and once the initial Servette attacks had been stifled, Derby had produced the more controlled football and began to look the more likely team to score.

Within thirty seconds of the restart, Derby had equalised and effectively killed the tie, having cancelled out the Servette away goal. A Rioch cross from the left should have been easy for the goalkeeper to collect but he fumbled the ball and dropped at the feet of Lee who shoved it into the net. From now onwards, as the final result became inevitable, the Swiss team began kicking out, with Morgenegg (who had a reputation for being a ruthless defender) and substitute Barriquand being the main culprits.

On seventy-two minutes a thunderous Rioch free kick from just outside the penalty area could not be held by de Blaireville who pushed the ball out to Bourne, his shot being parried. Hector was following up and casually nodded into the unguarded net. By this time the Servette sweeper, Guyot, had been playing as a forward in the second-half and Boulton had been forced to save from him on two occasions, one that he tipped onto the post. The game was over as a contest and some wayward shooting from the Derby forwards prevented the scoreline from being more emphatic.

Jeff Bourne seemed to be singled out by several Servette players, including Morgenegg, and it was getting him rattled. The only sign of annoyance came from Hector who threw the ball away following another poor refereeing decision and was promptly booked.

Another bonus from the trip off the field was that Roy McFarland started kicking a ball again during the training sessions before the game. Mackay said of his captain, 'We must be patient for his sake.' Starting tentatively, he became more confident and even played in a five-a-side game. McFarland was also upbeat, 'It's not now a case of if I come back to football, but when.'

After the first round, Derby were the only English club left in the competition and were the first name out of the hat in the draw for the second round; they were followed by the hardest team in the competition – Atlético Madrid, the tie of the round. Mackay commented, 'I don't believe we could have been drawn against a harder side, nor more attractive opposition. If they come to chop, then we can be hard, too.'

ATLÉTICO MADRID

The previous year they were the European Cup finalists, losing
to Bayern Munich after a replay in the final. They had played
Celtic in the semi-final in a bad-tempered affair that saw three
Atlético players sent off in the first leg – it was reported as one of
the worst cases of cynical fouling the tournament had seen. Their
coach was Juan Carlos Lorenzo who became famous as the Argentina
manager during the 1966 World Cup finals where Sir Alf Ramsey called his
teams 'animals' following the display against England.

23 October 1974
Second round, first leg
Derby County 2–2 Atlético Madrid
Derby County: Boulton, Webster, Nish, Rioch, Daniel, Todd, Newton, Gemmill,
Bourne (sub Hinton 65 mins), Hector, Lee
Atlético Madrid: Reina, Capón, Díaz, Marcelino (sub Bermejo 65 mins), Benegas,
Eusebio, Leal (sub Luis Aragonés 78 mins), Adelardo, Gárate, Irureta, Ayala
Referee: Mr Roger Helles (France)
Attendance: 29,347

The previous weekend had seen Derby slip to an unexpected 3–0 defeat at Carlisle
United, with Colin Boulton dropping two high crosses to allow the home side to
score. That defeat left them in sixth place in the league, whereas a win would have
taken them up to third.

Derby kicked towards the Osmaston End in the first half. One of the points noted
by Mackay and chief scout Bert Johnson was that the Spanish defence at times tended
to be ball-watching and in the early stages this was exploited from a Derby corner
taken by Gemmill. His centre found Nish all alone but his shot went over the bar.
After just thirteen minutes, however, Atlético scored the first goal following a long
kick out from the goalkeeper Reina. Webster and Gárate jumped for the ball and
the ball ended up at the feet of the Argentinian Ayala; from 30 yards out he hit a
powerful, dipping volley that beat Boulton.

Within a minute Derby equalised when a Gemmill corner was partially cleared
by Reina and the ball came out to Nish whose half-hit shot must have come through
a crowd of players as it left the goalkeeper flummoxed and flat-footed. The last half
an hour of the game saw some odd refereeing decisions. The first one should have
resulted in a penalty to Derby when a defender, challenged by Hector, handled
the ball in the area – the referee gave Derby an indirect free kick instead of the
expected penalty.

In the seventy-eighth minute, however, he did give a penalty albeit when there was
no obvious offence at all – this time to Atlético. Bermejo cleared a Derby attack that
set Gárate clear. As he chased the ball, it appeared he tripped Webster to get a run on
goal. Boulton rushed from goal and dived at the feet of the forward, grabbing the ball
at the second attempt. Inexplicably the referee, who was some way behind the play,

RAM

10p

Official Programme

the Official Newspaper of DERBY COUNTY F.C.

Weds, Oct 23, 1974 (UEFA Cup, Second Round, First Leg v Atletico Madrid, k.o. 7.30 p.m.) Vol. 4 Number Seven.

Derby County, November 1974: Back row, left to right: Gordon Guthrie (physiotherapist), Rod Thomas, Peter Daniel, Ron Webster, Graham Moseley, Colin Boulton, Alan Hinton, Colin Todd, David Nish, Kevin Hector, Des Anderson (asst. manager/chief coach).
Front: Roger Davies, Jeff Bourne, Archie Gemmill, Roy McFarland, Mr Stuart Webb (Secretary), Mr Sam Longson (Chairman), Mr Dave Mackay (Manager), Francis Lee, Steve Powell, Henry Newton, Bruce Rioch.

It's going to be tough

BACK AGAIN tonight to European football . . . and what a challenge this time for Derby County. Visitors in this Second Round, first leg UEFA Cup tie are last season's beaten European Champion's Cup finalists Atletico from Madrid.

Without doubt, the Spaniards are one of the finest sides in all Europe. And one of the most difficult to beat.

But highflying Rams, doing so well in the First Division after an indifferent start, and earning high praise for their all-out attacking football which is bringing more and more goals and exciting entertainment as the team blends together, hope and expect to do well in this vital first leg where a Derby lead of at least two goals is absolutely essential.

On top of that, it's almost a year since manager Dave Mackay took over, a year of which he can be proud.

"We've come a long way in that year, this match will provide us with the real clue as to where we stand in the context of European football.

"Two years ago Der-

TWO GOAL LEAD (AT LEAST) IS VITAL TO HOLD THIS FABULOUS ATLETICO MADRID

by County reached the semi-finals of the European Cup, beating such fine sides as Benfica and Trnava on the way. But the defensive techniques of Juventus from Italy brought their downfall.

"Possibly Atletico are even harder and tougher at the back. Our increased goalpower in League football is one thing. Now we have to overcome packed defence in depth, and tactics and style, to which our lads are not accustomed. As we burst forward looking for goals we shall have to watch carefully for Atletico's counter-strikes where they are so dangerous.

"It's going to be a fascinating match. That's for sure."

One thing else, for sure, is that the Spaniards will be giving extra special attention to ebullient Francis Lee and will take special

care to watch Bruce Rioch around the box where he is now becoming so lethal.

Big disappointment for Manager Mackay is the fact that Derby came out of the hat first in this tie, and so have to play first at home. For Roger Davies is still not able to play in Europe . . . he was suspended for three matches following his sending off against Juventus in the second leg of the European Cup semi-final at the Baseball Ground a year last April. This is the third match and he will be available, if selected, in Madrid.

"Roger's height and heading ability was what we wanted in the home leg," says the Manager, "but we must not cry crocodile tears

about it. We might as well wish Roy McFarland was available but, then, Peter Daniel is playing so well."

So, the scene is set for one of the most exciting games ever witnessed at the Baseball Ground. It's vital Rams get a two-goal lead, at least, if they are to survive.

"We formulated certain tactics as a result of all this activity," says Dave Mackay who takes his squad to a secret hideout the night before the match.

Atletico on the telly

NOTHING COULD have been more thorough than Derby County's preparation for the game with Atletico Madrid. On Sunday chief scout Bert Johnson watched them in their League game against Real Zaragoza in Spain and on Monday he joined the Rams' squad for team talks at ATV's Birmingham studios where everyone watched the film of Atletico's European Cup final games with Bayern Munich of West Germany when they were first held to a 1-1 draw through a last-minute Bayern goal, and then beaten 4-nill in the replay.

WIN A FREE FLIGHT TO MADRID

HERE'S your chance to travel with Derby County's team to Madrid for the second leg of tonight's UEFA Cup match with Atletico. And you travel FREE.

Derby County Promotions are offering fans an unbelievable opportunity to fly out with the official party.

All we are asking you to do is to sign on for Derby County Promotions's special "team" . . . of agents to sell the new Baseball Bonanaza tickets. To qualify you have to promise to sell just ten tickets — yes, ten!

Get your application in, to Derby County Promotions at 55 Osmaston Road, Derby: by first post next Saturday, October 26, and you will qualify for the draw which will be made at the Middlesbrough match.

A SUS AMIGOS ESPAGNOL

Los jugadores, la dirrecion y los seguidores del club Derby County les dan a sus amigos Espagnol que Atletico Madrid la bienvenida a los partidos de la Copa UEFA en "The Baseball Ground". Estamos seguros de que resultaran mas amistades Continentales, consolidando los lazos ya establecidos desde hace dos temporadas cuando llegamos hasta las semifinales de la Copa de Europa. Agradecemos la oportunidad de visitar sus paises respectivos y de llegar a conocernos mejor.

TO OUR SPANISH FRIENDS

Derby County players, management and supporters welcome our Spanish friends from Atletico Madrid to UEFA Cup matches at the Baseball Ground. We feel confident that more friendships from the Continent will be made, extending the links already established when we reached the European Cup semi-finals two seasons ago. We welcome the chance to visit your country to get the opportunity to know more about you.

The programme from the home leg against Atlético Madrid.

ran up to the players and pointed to the penalty spot, which came as shock to both sets of players as there appeared to have been no foul and there was no appeal from the Spanish team. Leal, who had an excellent game until that point was substituted to allow a specialist penalty taker, Luis Aragonés, to come on and score with his first kick. This incident seemed to rattle Derby for a period of time as Boulton was called upon to make two further good saves from Gárate and Capón to keep Derby in the tie.

The introduction of Hinton meant that Derby's attacks were more direct and his wide position and ability to send over pinpoint crosses from any position and to shoot accurately gave a new dimension to the play. It also made the previously calm defenders begin to panic whenever he had the ball. Two minutes from the end the referee balanced up the strange penalty decisions by giving one to Derby. Lee, his back to goal, waiting for his marker Eusebio to get close, went down in a most theatrical fashion. Rioch took the responsibility for the kick at the Normanton End and put the ball to the goalkeeper's left-hand side, right into the corner to make the score 2–2 on the night.

Hinton, on as a substitute for Bourne, nearly won the game when he reminded everyone of his skill by beating two defenders on the left, cut inside and fired a shot that hit a post and bounced out. However, the score ended as 2–2, with Atlético being the happier with the result, knowing that they had also scored two away goals with the home leg to come.

Derby's best players were probably Daniel and Todd in the centre of the defence, an indication that they had to be on alert all the time to cover the movement, pace and skill of the opposition forwards.

There was still hope for Derby as, looking at the history books and despite Atlético reaching the European Cup Final in the previous season, the Spaniards had only won one European game at home, with their best performances always reserved for the away ties. Dave Mackay said that the first leg was 'a triumph for pure football, I am convinced we are far from out of it yet as they have rarely done as well at home as away in European competition,' a view that was echoed by the Spanish media. Derby had to go to Spain and either win outright or have a high-scoring draw (at least 3–3) – a 2–2 draw would send the game into extra time and any other result would mean an aggregate victory for the Spanish team.

6 November 1974
Second round, second leg
Atlético Madrid 2–2 Derby County (4–4 on aggregate, Derby won 7–6 on penalties)
Atlético Madrid: Reina, Capón, Díaz, Adelardo (sub Marcelino 45 mins),
Benegas, Eusebio, Alberto (sub Salcedo 61 mins), Luis, Gárate, Irureta, Ayala
Derby County: Boulton, Webster, Nish, Rioch, Daniel, Powell, Newton,
Gemmill, Davies, Hector, Lee
Referee: Mr F. Biwersl (West Germany)
Attendance: 35,000

From the first leg Derby knew that Atlético were a talented side who would defend in numbers when required and break dangerously when under pressure. Both teams could be equally confident of making progress in the competition, although Atlético

Poster advertising the Atlético game.

had the advantage with two away goals. Derby had had mixed results in the league since the first leg; first Middlesbrough won 3–2 at the Baseball Ground but the week after the Rams won 1–0 at Leeds United with a late Francis Lee goal; it was Derby's first win at Elland Road since December 1946. Derby would be without their best defender Todd who had been absent since the first leg and was replaced by Powell to play alongside Daniel. Gemmill would make his 200th appearance for the club in the Vicente Calderón Stadium in Madrid.

Derby needed to avoid an early goal against them and to silence the home crowd, but they got off to the worst possible start; after just four minutes Gemmill fouled Ayala near the goal line and Adelardo chipped over the free kick for Luis, who lost his marker to head unopposed past Boulton. After this huge setback, Derby had opportunities in the remainder of the first half to go in ahead at the break, exploiting the frailties in the Atlético defence that were evident in the first leg. Firstly, Lee was put clear by Gemmill but took the ball too wide when he went round the goalkeeper. Then Rioch found himself in the penalty area when a cross from Nish picked him out but his shot went harmlessly over the bar.

Derby had to score at least twice in the second half and Gemmill was in total control of the midfield area and was pushing Derby forward at every opportunity with some flowing moves. Even Daniel got a shot on goal in the opening stages that was blocked by the goalkeeper's legs before the game took a new twist on fifty-four minutes – Hector's cross was neatly headed down by Davies for Rioch to run onto and push into the net from close range. With twenty-five minutes to go Derby took the lead for the first time in the two legs when Lee went past Diaz's tackle and knocked the ball back for Gemmill to cross. Hector had time and space to chest the ball down and shoot first time into the net. Newton almost added a third goal when he exchanged passes with Francis Lee and his shot clipped the outside of a post.

Twelve minutes from time, Newton was involved again as he was harshly penalised for a hand ball on the edge of the penalty area. Luis, the Atlético dead-ball specialist, took the kick and bent his effort into the net, giving Boulton no chance. The scores were now 4–4 overall, cancelling out the away goals scored by both teams, and the only scoreline that would see the game go into extra time.

Extra time was a predictably cagey affair and the longer it went on, the more defensive it became. Inevitably, penalties were required to decide the winner. This was Derby's first ever participation in a penalty shoot-out and their nominated takers were Rioch, Hector, Davies, Nish and Lee, with the Rams kicking first. Rioch and Hector were successful with their kicks, as was Luis and Ayala for Atlético. Roger Davies then saw his effort saved by Reina who dived away to his left before Salcedo put the Spaniards ahead 3–2, with two penalties to go. Nish levelled the score and then Capón lifted his kick over the bar to square things up again. The last two kicks were converted, leaving the penalty score at 4–4 and the game moved into a sudden-death scenario. Gemmill's and Newton's kicks were converted and were matched by Benegas and Gárate. Powell, who had a tremendous game in the centre of defence, scored his kick and Boulton then dived to his right to push Eusebio's kick against a post, with the ball staying out. Eusebio ran in and scored the rebound but to no avail.

It was now nearly midnight in Madrid as the game finished; it was a draining experience, both physically and emotionally, for all concerned including the fans at home, listening to the penalties on the Radio 2/Radio Derby commentary.

In the post-match press conference the Atlético manager, Lorenzo, said, 'Whoever expected an English team to attack . . . attack like Derby did here . . . we've gone out to the best English side we have ever seen.'

In the third round draw Derby had to wait until last as they watched all the other ties being drawn before theirs. They were drawn against the Yugoslav team Velež Mostar. The two teams drawn immediately before them were the two to be avoided – Juventus and Ajax.

Velež Mostar

27 November 1974
Third round, first leg
Derby County 3–1 Velež Mostar
Derby County: Boulton, Webster, Nish, Rioch,
Daniel, Todd, Newton, Gemmill, Davies (sub Bourne
59 mins), Hector, Lee (sub Hinton 69 mins)
Velež Mostar: Mrgan, Čolić, Hadžiabdić, Primorac,
Glavović, Pecell, Topić, Vladić (sub Okuka 61 mins), Vokole, Ledic, Hodzic
Referee: Mr P. Mannig (East Germany)
Attendance: 26,131

Colin Todd had recovered from his injury and his replacement, Steve Powell, found himself unluckily left out of the starting eleven. The goal areas were covered in mud and there is no doubt that had this been a league game, the match would have been postponed. Mistakes on both sides were inevitable and defenders would have to be careful about playing the ball out and goalkeepers wary of the greasy ball.

Derby found themselves a goal down after just two minutes and twenty-two seconds when Hadžiabdić was allowed to run forward and eventually played a cross-field ball out to the captain Topić on the right side. He took on Nish and then crossed into the centre. Todd was there to stop the initial ball, but it bounced away from him straight into the path of Vladić who was following up to shoot firmly past Boulton. Whatever plans Derby had made before the start of the game had to be rewritten quickly. Having secured the away goal the Velež team could concentrate on defending that lead and launching counter-attacks as Derby pressed forwards.

It was clear that Velež had plenty of skilful players in the midfield area, particularly Vladić and Topić, but, as the game progressed the lone forward, Vukoje, became increasingly isolated. That did not mean that the Derby defence could take it easy, however, as he was always looking to control the ball, wait for team-mates to join him and turn and run. It was one of the breaks – a Topić through-ball that set Vukoje free and clear – that led to Daniel bringing him down just outside the area; Vladić's free kick was touched over the bar by Boulton.

The programme from the home leg against Velež.

Derby had their opportunities in the first half with Lee just missing a low cross from Hector and the same player putting a shot over the bar when Davies nodded down a Nish corner. As the second half began, Derby predictably poured forward but the central defensive partnership of Primorac and Glavović seemed capable of handling what Derby were throwing at them. Mackay made two crucial substitutions in the game by introducing Bourne for Davies on the hour and, ten minutes later, Hinton for Lee. With nineteen minutes to play Derby were still trailing by that early goal but the combination of Bourne and Hinton gave the Velež defence problems that they struggled to overcome.

After seventy-four minutes the Rams were level. Rioch intercepted a throw on the Velež left and crossed for Bourne who initially headed down to Hector. Hector immediately played the ball back for Bourne to head it unchallenged into the net, scoring his first goal of the season.

With ten minutes left to play, a good move involving Rioch, Bourne and Webster down Derby's right flank allowed Webster to clip the ball to the edge of the penalty area where Hinton ran in front of the centre-half to win the ball. With his back to goal, in one movement he turned to his right giving him that little bit of space he required, and curled a left-foot shot into the top right-hand corner of Mrgan's goal.

'I don't think I've ever scored a better goal,' he said afterwards. That was to be the last goal he would score in his Derby County career.

Another poor throw from the Velež defender near the corner flag allowed Gemmill to intercept on the edge of the area. He ran forwards at pace and his low centre was swept into the net by Bourne past the despairing dive of the keeper and just inside the post.

Derby pushed forwards again and Hector slammed the ball into the net following a goalmouth scramble, but it was disallowed for a push by Hinton as he tried to get through. There was also time for the Velež giant defender Glavović to be sent off for headbutting Bourne.

One note of concern was a late injury to Nish when he slid across the mud and straight into the small wall that surrounded the Paddock terracing. Gordon Guthrie was on hand immediately to attend. Initial reports suggested a damaged ankle and this would keep him out of the team for a month.

In the end it was the substitutions that caused panic in the Velež defence and allowed the recovery to a 3–1 advantage after the first leg. However, Derby would be aware of the quality of the Velež players and they had to produce another performance like the one in the second half in Madrid.

The East German referee booked Vladić (for a foul on Rioch) and Ledic (for kicking the ball away) and they were joined in the book in the second half by Topić (a foul on Gemmill) and Alan Hinton who had come onto the field without permission.

11 December 1974
Third round, second leg
Velež Mostar 4–1 Derby County (Derby lose 5–4 on aggregate)
Velež Mostar: Mrgan, Meter, Hadžiabdić, Čolić, Primorac, Pecelj, Topić,
Halilhodžić, Bajevic, Vladić, Vukoje
Derby County: Boulton, Webster, Thomas, Rioch, Daniel, Todd, Newton,
Gemmill, Bourne (sub Davies 55 mins), Hector, Lee (sub Hinton 73 mins)
Referee: Mr C. Corver (Holland)
Attendance: 15,000

Derby's only game following on from the home leg was a creditable 2–2 draw at
Liverpool, with the game on 30 November against Wolverhampton Wanderers being
postponed because of the state of the Baseball Ground pitch.

The team and many of the supporters were staying in Dubrovnik for four days
and all were well looked after. The pitch in Mostar was wet and greasy on top,
as you would expect in December and the reception in the town was cold and,
in the stadium, extremely hostile. Derby had conceded early goals in their last
two European matches and were desperately keen not to do the same in Mostar.
They were full of nerves at the start with Newton and Thomas colliding. Gemmill
then failed to clear an attack and let the ball get away from him; in trying to win
it back, he brought down Vukoje in the penalty area. Primorac took the resulting
penalty and although Boulton got a hand to it, he could not prevent the shot from
going in. Velež scored again after half an hour bringing the aggregate scores level,
with the advantage of an away goal; Boulton punched away a Vladić corner and
that clearance fell to Pecelj standing on the edge of the area – his shot was drilled
through the crowded goalmouth and into the net.

Half time came and allowed management to reassess the situation. In the first half
Derby constantly lost possession and rarely looked like creating a positive move.
Vladić was causing Derby all sorts of problems and there appeared to be nothing that
could stop him. Things got worse in the second half when a bizarre goal gave Velež a
3–0 lead; a Vladić free kick came back off the crossbar and hit Boulton on his back to
trickle over the line.

For a while Derby were rattled and Daniel (tripping Vladić), Hector (dissent,
meaning he would miss the next European tie as he had been booked against
Servette), Newton and Todd were all booked along with Halilhodžić and Čolić of
Velež. Mackay sent Davies on in place of Bourne in the fifty-fifth minute and it had an
immediate effect. Newton crossed from the left for Davies to nod down into Hector's
path who forced his way between two defenders to score. Only then did Derby begin
to play – in the last thirty minutes Velež began to look shaky and introduced some
illegal tactics.

Newton hit a post with a superb drive from 20 yards that went through a crowded
penalty area but the rebound came out to Davies too quickly for him to react and get
in a firm shot, instead hitting it wide. Newton also had another shot go narrowly over
the bar and Hector had a shot cleared off the line. At this stage the scores were level
at 4–4 with both away goals having been cancelled out. Extra time again looked the
most likely outcome.

Disaster struck on eighty-six minutes when a shot from Hadžiabdić was directed at Colin Todd at close range, hitting him on the shoulder. Referee Corver saw it as a hand ball offence and gave the penalty kick. Derby's protests were waved away as Bajavic scored and there was no time left to get back. It was a cruel end for the team, especially after their second-half display. However, it was a tie that should have been straightforward following the home leg. The headline in the *Guardian* was 'Derby penalised out of Cup' and Mackay remembers, 'that night in Mostar was the saddest of my career.'

Derby made an official protest to UEFA and actually appeared in the draw for the next round (v FC Twente of Holland) while the appeal was under way. Despite media reports, Derby's protest did not make a formal request for a replay of the second leg. The official protest made four points:

1) Derby actually kicked off both halves of the game, under the instructions of referee Corver

2) Pelecj was allowed to leave the field for treatment and come back to play without the referee's permission. The same player had already been booked for foul play and should therefore have been sent off. Hinton was booked for entering the field as a substitute in the home leg without getting permission

3) Mackay and the rest of the staff complained of threats and stone-throwing at them during the game

4) Intimidation of fire-crackers, smoke flares aimed at the Derby keeper . . . despite various tannoy announcements for crowd control had no effect. Even the Velež captain left the field to make a personal plea to the crowd. They felt strongly that they upset the players and influenced the referee, particularly for the late penalty decision against Todd for hand ball.

The original decision by UEFA was that the case was not proved at their Control and Disciplinary Committee on 22 January 1975 and Derby launched an immediate appeal. Velež were fined 3,000 Swiss Francs for the firing of rockets and fire-crackers during the game but Derby ultimately failed and were ordered to pay the costs of the hearing.

The appeal was to be held on 14 February 1975 in Zurich but would only accept photos of any of the incidents to support the claim. Stuart Webb, Frank Innes, Mackay and Gemmill represented the club at this hearing and reference to Borussia Mönchengladbach v Inter Milan in the 1971/72 season was made where similar circumstances occurred.

Mackay said at the hearing, 'Stones were thrown at myself and the Derby County substitutes. I found the whole matter very disturbing . . . I have never experienced anything like the rocket-firing and the intimidation by the Velež supporters during the game.'

Gemmill also made a statement, 'I personally felt that the referee was under undue strain as well as myself and my players by the crowd's violent actions and

Derby's appeal team get ready to board their plane at East Midlands airport.

intimidation. I have never experienced anything like the situation that faced my team and myself in Velež.'

This appeal was also rejected on the grounds that there was no new evidence presented and the firing of the rockets had no bearing on the actual match result.

UEFA Cup 1974/75

First round

18 September 1974	Derby County 4–1 Servette Geneva	
2 October 1974	Servette Geneva 1–2 Derby County	(W 6–2 on agg)

Second round

23 October 1974   Derby County 2–2 Atlético Madrid
6 November 1974   Atlético Madrid 2–2 Derby County
                                   (4–4 on aggregate, Derby won 7–6 on penalties)

Third round

27 November1974	Derby County 3–1 Velež Mostar	
11 December 1974	Velež Mostar 4–1 Derby County	(L 5–4 on agg)

European Cup 1975/76

Top ten Division One, 1974/75

Team	P	W	D	L	F	A	W	D	L	F	A	Pts
Derby County	42	14	4	3	41	18	7	7	7	26	31	53
Liverpool	42	14	5	2	44	17	6	6	9	16	22	51
Ipswich Town	42	17	2	2	47	14	6	3	12	19	30	51
Everton	42	10	9	2	33	19	6	9	6	23	23	50
Stoke City	42	12	7	2	40	18	5	8	8	24	30	49
Sheffield United	42	12	7	2	35	20	6	6	9	23	31	49
Middlesbrough	42	11	7	3	33	14	7	5	9	21	26	48
Manchester City	42	16	3	2	40	15	2	7	12	14	39	46
Leeds United	42	10	8	3	34	20	6	5	10	23	29	45
Burnley	42	11	6	5	40	29	6	5	10	28	38	45

There were some notable teams involved in the competition and it was important not to draw any of the main contenders in the early rounds – Juventus, Benfica, Real Madrid, Bayern Munich, Rangers, St Etienne and PSV Eindhoven.

There was an added incentive this year as the final would be played at Hampden Park which would ensure a large number of Derby fans to witness it, should they get that far. In the first round Slovan Bratislava, the Czechoslovakian champions, were drawn out of the hat with the first leg being played in Bratislava. They were no pushover either; Bratislava had played five home legs in the European Cup since their first entry in 1956 and had won every single one and lost only two of the seventeen home European matches played so far.

SLOVAN BRATISLAVA

17 September 1975
First round, first leg
Slovan Bratislava 1–0 Derby County
Slovan Bratislava: Vencel, Pivarník, Ondruš, Jozef
Čapkovič, Gögh, Medvid, Pekarik (sub Haraslin),
Novotny, Masný, Švehlík, Jan Čapkovič
Derby County: Boulton, Thomas, Todd, McFarland,
Nish, Powell, Newton, Gemmill, Rioch, Lee (sub Bourne), George
Referee: Mr K. Ohmsen (West Germany)
Attendance: 45,000

Derby came into the game in a good run of form having won their last three matches – 3–0 v Burnley, 2–1 v Huddersfield Town in the League Cup and a 3–2 win at Tottenham Hotspur – although prior to this game they had only scored four goals in their last seven away matches. They were lying in eighth place, level on points with Liverpool and three points behind the early season leaders Manchester United and West Ham United.

Hector was serving the first of his two-match European suspension and as a defensive measure Powell replaced him, making his first appearance of the season in a more rigid 4–4–2 formation. They had to learn from the last two away legs they had played in when they conceded early goals and were on the back foot for over half the game, surviving one tie on penalties and losing the other. Boulton was a doubt before the game but came through a fitness test in the morning so was able to play.

The formation worked well in the first half and by counter-attacking, Derby made three clear-cut chances which were not taken. After only ten minutes Lee was pushed in the back and Newton tapped the free kick square only for Rioch to see his shot hit the foot of a post with Vencel in the Slovan goal beaten. Francis Lee then turned on a throw from Gemmill, and hit a shot from long range which Vencel fumbled.

Slovan were quiet in the first half and Derby were happy at the break with a 0–0 scoreline. Just into the second half, an error by Gögh let Charlie George through, but Vencel came out and managed to kick the shot away to safety. Had George scored at that point, it would have been no more than they deserved as the home fans started to get more and more critical. Lee and George were running miles up front, but as the pressure mounted on Derby's defence the midfield struggled to get the ball up to them.

Ten minutes later the game was turned around. Čapkovič took a corner, Švehlík flicked it on and Masný was there to prod the ball past Boulton. For the last thirty minutes it was Slovan who dominated the game and had further chances to increase the lead. A header from Ondruš from another corner almost got through a crowd of players, while a Pivarnik dipping shot was well saved by Boulton and Masný scraped the post with another effort. Throughout the increasing pressure on the Derby goal, Roy McFarland was always on hand to clear the ball with boot or head and nothing was getting past him.

Medzinárodné futbalové stretnutie

O POHÁR MAJSTROV EURÓPSKYCH KRAJÍN

SLOVAN CHZJD BRATISLAVA

DERBY COUNTY

Štadión Slovana na Tehelnom poli

17. septembra 1975 ∗   19.30 hod.

The programme from the away leg against Slovan, the most common and easily obtainable programme from Derby's European away games.

There were some excellent performances from the Derby players especially Powell who came into midfield, and alongside him Newton, who probably had his best game for Derby – they had a stranglehold on the game in the first half. The other star was McFarland, who was back to his best after a year out with injury. Les Cocker, the England assistant manager, was watching from the stands with a view to England's forthcoming fixture in the same stadium in the coming months. In the end a 1–0 defeat was considered a good result and on the evidence of the first half especially, there were weaknesses in the Slovan defence that could be exploited and the feeling was that the Czechoslovakians had missed their opportunity. Not that the return game would be easy, as fans would remember Spartak Trnava from the same country a couple of years earlier who Derby struggled to overturn a similar scoreline.

1 October 1975
First round, second leg
Derby County 3–0 Slovan Bratislava (Derby win 3–1 on aggregate)
Derby County: Boulton, Thomas, Nish, Ricoh, McFarland, Todd, Newton (sub Bourne 35 mins), Gemmill, Lee, Hector, George
Slovan Bratislava: Vencel, Elefant, Jozef Čapkovič, Ondruš, Gögh, Medvid (sub Haraslin 45 mins), Masný, Švehlík, Pekarik, Novotny, Jan Čapkovič
Referee: Mr L. Van der Kroft (Holland)
Attendance: 30,888

Since the first leg Derby had beaten both Manchester teams at home and suffered a 1–0 defeat at Stoke City, leaving them in sixth place in Division One. They were still three points behind the new leaders, Queens Park Rangers, who had stunned Derby on the opening day of the season by winning 5–1 at the Baseball Ground on the newly laid turf.

Derby were kicking towards the Normanton End in the first half and for all the possession they had, were restricted to long-range efforts at goal, which were dealt with comfortably by the goalkeeper. Charlie George, picking up a flick on from Francis Lee hit one from twenty-five yards that was straight at the keeper and then Hector skipped through a challenge to set Gemmill running down the left and just as it seemed as he was going to cross the ball from the corner of the penalty area, he hit a shot towards the near post that the goalkeeper beat away.

A Nish corner didn't get very high and went through McFarland and two defenders at the near post, falling to George eight yards out; his shot, however, was blocked on the line and the rebound evaded Hector. Apart from these incidents, the Slovan defence was coping and they were able to pass the ball and move to create space and angles to allow them to keep the ball for periods of time.

Derby were forced to make a substitution on thirty-five minutes when Newton came out of a tackle with a twisted ankle and, although he tried to carry on, he was clearly struggling. Mackay might have been tempted to let him run it off until half time, but decided to replace him straight away with Bourne coming on. This meant that a change in formation was necessary with Bourne taking up a wide position and running forward moves from deep, which the Slovan defence did not master. Instead of high balls being kicked upfield to George and Lee, more constructive attacks started to take place with Bourne in plenty of space.

The programme from the home leg against Slovan.

Francis Lee scores on eighty-two minutes.

As half time approached, Derby scored the goal that brought the aggregate scores level. A cross into the penalty area from Rioch from the left was partially headed out to Gemmill on the right, with Bourne to his left unmarked and wanting the ball. Gemmill controlled the ball and cut inside the defender who brought him down. The ball had broken to Bourne 20 yards out and in a central position. He hit the ball first time all along the ground past the goalkeeper and it bounced into the goal off the post. The half-time mood was buoyant and with the aggregate scores level, Derby had forty-five minutes to score one more goal.

The pattern was set as Derby pushed forward relentlessly, with Rioch and Gemmill involved in everything. A long kick downfield from Boulton was flicked on by George to Lee who laid it off to Bourne on the left wing. He rolled the ball invitingly for Rioch thirty-five yards out and his thunderbolt shot was on target but towards the centre of the goal so Vencel was able to touch it over the bar – a foot either side and he would not have been able to stop it.

A corner kick from Hector on sixty-six minutes from the right was too deep and was headed clear as far as David Nish whose shot bounced through everyone and hit the post with the goalkeeper stationary.

With twelve minutes to go, Derby finally took the lead when Lee received a pass from Colin Todd some thirty yards from goal. He had time to control the ball, turn and, with the defenders backing off, he was able to shoot along the ground past Vencel and into the bottom corner of the net. Just two minutes later, Gemmill burst forward and played the ball out to Bourne on the left in some space. He played the ball first time for Gemmill to run onto, where he was shadowed by Ondruš. As Gemmill took him on towards the goal line, Ondruš brought him down and the referee did not hesitate in giving the penalty. Francis Lee took a long run-up to the ball and hit it straight and low but as the goalkeeper dived to his left, he was able to clear the ball with his feet.

On eighty-two minutes Nish skipped through numerous Slovan players to try to beat the offside trap but lost the ball on the edge of the area; fortunately for him Elefant tried to pass back to the goalkeeper but it was intercepted by Nish who tried to knock it past the onrushing Vencel. The initial shot was blocked but came out to Lee who shoved it into the net with glee.

There was still time for another opportunity when good play from Nish and Bourne set Hector away down the right wing and his firm cross was met by Lee. When his first attempt was blocked by Vencel, Lee was first to his feet, six yards out and the goalkeeper on the floor. Somehow, however, he managed to scoop the shot over the bar – it was a good job that the tie had been won by that stage.

It had been a fine all-round performance with Nish (who had stifled the threat of Masný) and Bourne (who had been on the transfer list for some weeks with no interest shown in his services) standing out in a thrilling match that was not settled until the last ten minutes when Derby's persistence finally wore down the Slovan defence.

REAL MADRID

Bringing these two teams together at the Baseball Ground seemed unthinkable twenty years earlier when Derby were having to battle their way out of Division Three (North) while Real Madrid were winning their first European Cup. This match, in terms of glamour, expectation and excitement, eclipsed that of the Benfica visit three years earlier.

22 October 1975
Second round, first leg
Derby County 4–1 Real Madrid
Derby County: Boulton, Thomas, Nish, Rioch, McFarland, Todd, Newton, Gemmill, Lee, Hector (sub Bourne 79 mins), George (sub Davies 79 mins)
Real Madrid: Miguel Ángel, Sol, Rubiñan, Pirri, Camacho, Velázquez, Amancio, Breitner, Del Bosque, Netzer, Martinez
Referee: Mr A. Ivonhal (Russia)
Attendance: 34,839

Since the first-round win against Slovan Bratislava, there had been two home wins (1–0 v Ipswich Town and 3–2 v Wolverhampton Wanderers) and a 0–0 draw at Norwich City that had left the Rams in seventh place in the table; there was also a 1–0 defeat away at Middlesbrough in the third round of the League Cup. In the Spanish league, Real Madrid had just drawn 1–1 away at Real Sociedad and were unbeaten so far with two draws and four victories. Among their star-studded team were two members of the 1974 World Cup-winning West German team – Paul Breitner and Günter Netzer – both signed in response to their arch-rivals Barcelona signing Johan Cruyff.

Sam Longson, the Derby chairman, at a banquet prior to the game said, 'Tonight we play the greatest name in European football . . . a great club from a great city. We are only a small club by comparison, but we have learned from your great achievements in the past, and we are envious of your great reputation for sportsmanship and honour.' What followed was an unforgettable game, probably one of the finest that the Baseball Ground staged during its 102 years as the home of Derby County Football Club. Real Madrid were in their change strip of all blue and Derby were attacking the Normanton End in the first half; Derby would be hoping to take a lead out to Madrid for the return.

After just ten minutes, Derby got the all-important first goal that raised the roof. A throw by Rod Thomas midway into the Real half (and in front of the Normanton Paddock) was thrown back to Todd on the halfway line. Although he was in lots of space and able to make progress forwards, he hit a superb cross-field ball to Nish, who was also in lots of space. He took two touches and knocked it wide where Gemmill had pulled out of the middle. The Real defence were not marking particularly closely and allowed him to take a touch to tee up the ball for a low, hard centre into the penalty area. The ball went behind Lee and Hector and was met by Charlie George near the penalty spot who was running across the face of the goal – his first-time, left-foot shot flew into the bottom corner of Miguel Ángel's goal. George ran away blowing kisses towards the Popside as Barry Davies on the *Sportnight* commentary screamed, 'That's a cracker . . . as good a first-time shot as you'll ever see . . . really brilliant goal!'

On seventeen minutes, a neat move between George, Hector and Lee was cleared for a throw, in front of the Popside, taken by Gemmill. He threw it back to Lee who turned his marker, Camacho, and ran into the penalty area. Lee was in front of the defender and appeared to be shaping to shoot when he fell to the ground. The referee had an unimpeded view of the incident and had no hesitation in awarding a penalty. George was to take the kick – his first for Derby; he took four steps and placed the ball with a right-foot shot high into the top-right of the Real Madrid net, with Ángel getting nowhere near the ball.

After a first twenty-five minutes in which they had been made to look very average, Real Madrid, sparked by Netzer, began a fightback and mounted pressure on the Derby goal. A strong run by Netzer came to Amancio who very nearly got away from Nish along the goal line, resulting in a corner. From the corner, which was partially cleared, Netzer passed back to Ángel who pushed it forwards to Amancio, who chipped over the Derby defence to Pirri; he was able to chest the ball down and slide it under Boulton. The way the Madrid players were now passing the ball among themselves would give Derby cause for concern. However, Derby had an indirect free kick inside the penalty area three minutes before half time and although this was eventually cleared, the pressure was kept up as McFarland brought the ball forwards from defence, over the halfway line, past Breitner, and he found Nish down the left-hand channel. Nish came inside and shot from just outside the penalty area. The goalkeeper appeared to have the ball covered, but the ball bounced just in front of him and somehow it went through his hands into the net, much to the delight of Nish and the fans.

As another Derby surge was halted on the edge of the Real penalty area, passes by Amancio, Martinez and Breitner pulled the Derby defence out of position allowing Pirri to collect the cross all alone and he slotted the ball past Boulton. There appeared to be nothing at all wrong with the goal, but the Russian linesman's flag went up for offside against Pirri, much to the horror of the Real players who surrounded him. This was not the first time this linesman had made a controversial decision – he was the man who confirmed that Geoff Hurst's shot had crossed the goal line after it hit the bar and bounced down during the 1966 World Cup final at Wembley. Davies and Bourne were ready to enter the action when Netzer's cross-field pass was intercepted by Gemmill on the halfway line and, via George, the ball ended up with Hector on the left wing in some space. He evaded the first tackle, but Netzer's tackle was deemed a foul by the referee and Derby were awarded a second penalty kick with twelve minutes to play. There followed a lengthy protest by many Real players surrounding the referee, but he stood firm on his decision having been only five yards away from the incident and perfectly placed.   George this time thumped the ball high and wide to the goalkeeper's left (while Ángel dived the opposite way) completing the first hat-trick in his career. A minute later George (who had picked up a knock at the start of the second half) and Hector were replaced by the waiting Davies and Bourne. There was still time for Ángel to make stunning saves from Rioch, Lee and Davies – the scoreline could easily have been 7–3.

It was a hugely impressive performance from the Derby team and although George took the headlines, it was Todd and Gemmill who laid the foundations. Gemmill did not look out of place among the World Cup-winning German midfielders and it was a mystery that he was unable to get into the Scottish squad recently announced by the manager Willie Ormond. A 4–1 scoreline was only half time in the tie, but should be enough to see them through to the next round. Real were unlucky on the night as they were unfortunate in the decision that gave Pirri offside and their play and movement certainly had the Derby defence stretched; it would surely be a long night in Madrid. Real made a significant contribution to the game by their fast, attacking football and were unfortunate in not scoring more themselves.

Derby could have been awarded two more penalties and Madrid had a goal disallowed and no-one, including Mackay, could understand why. However, this result was probably the greatest ever, eclipsing the 3–0 defeat of Benfica in 1972, as the Real team were of a much higher standard than the Portuguese on the night. Stuart Webb broadcast an appeal prior to the game for fans not to throw anything onto the pitch or to invade under any circumstances. This request originated from the UEFA observer Mr Luis Wooters, who was Chairman of Disciplinary Committee and was regarded as the toughest disciplinarian in UEFA – he said afterwards, 'I have not met a fairer crowd anywhere than those you had at the Baseball Ground.'

Sir Stanley Rous, who was the special guest, said that 'both clubs are led by men who insist on soccer as a sport and an entertainment. I am mighty proud to have been here tonight. There is hope for the world game when we can be so inspired by twenty-two players, by two managers, and by two sets of officials behind the scenes who want football first and foremost to be the winner.'

Mackay commented, 'You will never get another night like that one. That night was unbelievable and must rate as one of Derby's greatest results ever . . . I certainly consider it the best game I presided over as a manager. It was paralysing stuff – the best we have produced in Europe and Archie Gemmill gave the finest midfield display I've ever seen.'

It was the performance of the officials that most troubled the Madrid players. Gunter Netzer complained, 'We cannot win this match now and that is because of some terrible refereeing decisions,' while Paul Breitner said, 'I don't like to speak in bad ways about players or referees, but this referee through his poor decisions has taken away a whole year's hard work by our club. Our disallowed goal could not have been offside. Now I know how Leeds felt in Paris when a referee's decision cost them the final.' Madrid manager Miljan Miljanic said, 'we face a formidable task, but nothing is impossible for us at home.'

Charlie George's first goal was later voted the second best Derby County goal of all time as part of the 125th anniversary celebrations. For many who were at the game this goal was the best by some way.

5 November 1975
Second round, second leg
Real Madrid 5–1 Derby County (Derby lose 6–5 on aggregate)
Real Madrid: Miguel Ángel, Sol, Camacho, Pirri, Benito, Del Bosque, Amancio (sub Rubiñan 110 mins), Breitner, Santillana, Netzer, Roberto Martinez
Derby County: Boulton, Thomas, Nish, Powell, McFarland, Todd, Newton, Gemmill, Davies, Hector (sub Bourne 75 mins, sub Hinton 100 mins), George
Referee: Mr Hungerbuehler (Switzerland)
Attendance: 125,000

Given the attacking strength of Madrid, especially in front of a sell-out crowd at the Bernabéu, no-one was thinking the return leg would be a formality. Dave Mackay summed up the situation thus, 'if we can't hold a 4–1 lead, even against a side as good as Real are going to be without doubt on their own pitch, then we not deserve to survive.'

Exactly a year before the night, Derby played in the Vicente Calderón stadium, home of Atlético Madrid, so had the knowledge of the surroundings and noise that they would face. The weekend fixture had matched Derby at home to Leeds United and was the feature game on Match of the Day that evening. That particular game will live long in the memory as not only did it see Derby move up to fourth in the table a point behind Manchester United, it also saw a last-minute scorcher from Roger Davies and, most famously, the sending off of Derby's Francis Lee and Leeds' Norman Hunter for fighting.

During the football club's away games of the 1975/76 seaon, there had been a common theme – the inability to put the ball in the net, despite creating a number of chances. The rumblings of the German Günter Netzer went on some weeks after the tie had finished, believing that they had been badly treated by the referee in the first leg. There was a classic dilemma for manager Mackay – should he play his usual attacking formation despite leading 4–1 from the first leg, knowing that the Spaniards must win by at least three clear goals to stand a chance of going through? Or should he adopt a more defensive formation as he had in the away leg against Slovan Bratislava? Put another way, should he play a 4–3–3 formation with Rioch backing up Lee, George and Hector, or a 4–4–2 bringing in Steve Powell to replace one of the strikers? Some decisions were forced on Mackay – Lee was suspended and Rioch injured. On top of that the club doctor was flown out to Madrid as three other players – Newton, Powell and McFarland – all needed pain-killing injections and were doubtful even as the team arrived at the stadium. The team had a more defensive look about it, one forced on the manager and Hector was to play in a midfield position. The last thing Derby wanted was to concede an early goal, yet after only four minutes Real had scored. Netzer was inevitably involved when his chip in to Camacho was headed back into the penalty area where the ball dropped kindly for Martinez to score as the Derby defence hesitated. The pattern for the rest of the half had been set with Real launching attack after attack, inspired by the thirty-six-year-old Amancio, but the Spaniards could not find the net again before half time. By then the threat of Netzer had been cancelled out by Powell (who was booked for kicking the ball away at a free kick) and Newton and Derby would have been happy enough being a goal down at the break.

Within ten minutes of the restart the game had swung in Real's favour, with two goals. The first followed a free kick from Amancio that forced Boulton into a tremendous double save from Santillana, but the ball was finally bundled in by Martinez for his second goal of the game. With the huge crowd sensing more goals, the pressure continued and Powell gave away a free kick near the goal line. The kick was firmly headed in by Santillana who used his physical presence to get to the ball first. This brought the scores level on aggregate with Madrid having the advantage of the away goal. Derby now had to force the game and needed to score to stay in the competition.

After sixty-two minutes, as McFarland and Todd were being pushed further forward, Charlie George picked up a pass in a wide position, cut inside going past three tackles and hit a shot from twenty-five yards that curved and dipped before going into the net off the crossbar. This put Derby 5–4 ahead overall and this stayed the same until five minutes from the end. Amancio collected a brilliant pass from Netzer and he went down very easily under a challenge from Thomas to give Pirri the task of scoring from the resulting penalty kick, which he duly converted. Real boss Miljan Miljanic said, 'It was certainly not a penalty, but that unfortunately is football.' The players who were doubtful before the game were beginning to show the effects with McFarland limping, and nine minutes into the extra time period, Real scored again on a swift counter-attack – it was their best goal of the night. Santillana flicked the ball over his head and muscled his way between McFarland and Newton before hitting in a brilliant shot past Boulton. At this point Powell could hardly run and was about to be replaced when Camacho badly fouled Bourne who was carried off and this allowed Hinton to come on. Hinton was able to send over some superb crosses that had the Real defence in a panic. Davies could not quite reach one cross, Benito had to make a desperate clearance from another and McFarland shot over when well placed. However, Derby just couldn't score and afterwards the Real fans drove down the streets of the capital waving their flags and honking their horns in the typical Spanish manner.

Dave Mackay was gracious in defeat saying, 'Real played like world champions. They were superb. They played us off the park just as we did against them at Derby. We were cheated by that penalty six minutes from victory. The referees are mostly so bad that you will always be cheated in Europe. Real were cheated at Derby, but the blow came for us so close to the finish.'

The attendance at the Estadio Santiago Bernabéu of 120,000 remains the largest to ever watch a Derby County match. Charlie George said, sadly, 'I have scored four goals in this European Cup tie and we have still lost. Now, I'll have to score a couple at Highbury.' 'Rams Crash Out. Scintillating Santillana Sees Super Señors Home' screamed the headlines.

EUROPEAN CUP 1975/76

First round

17 September 1975	Slovan Bratislava 1–0 Derby County	
1 October 1975	Derby County 3–0 Slovan Bratislava	(W 3–1 on agg)

Second round

22 October 1975	Derby County 4–1 Real Madrid	
5 November 1975	Real Madrid 5–1 Derby County	(L 6–5 on agg)

UEFA Cup 1976/77

Top Ten Division One, 1975/76

Team	P	W	D	L	F	A	W	D	L	F	A	Pts
Liverpool	42	14	5	2	41	21	9	9	3	25	10	60
Queens Park Rangers	42	17	4	0	42	13	7	7	7	25	20	59
Manchester United	42	16	4	1	40	13	7	6	8	28	29	56
Derby County	42	15	3	3	45	30	6	8	7	30	28	53
Leeds United	42	13	3	5	37	19	8	6	7	28	27	51
Ipswich Town	42	11	6	4	36	23	5	8	8	18	25	46
Leicester City	42	9	9	3	29	24	4	10	7	19	27	45
Manchester City	42	14	5	2	46	18	2	6	13	18	28	43
Tottenham Hotspur	42	6	10	5	33	32	8	5	8	30	31	43
Norwich City	42	10	5	6	33	26	6	5	10	25	32	42

There were some big names in the UEFA Cup competition this season including FC Porto, Ajax, Manchester United, Barcelona, Celtic, Inter Milan, Feyenoord, AC Milan, Manchester City and Juventus. The pick of the first-round ties were Ajax against Manchester United and Manchester City against Juventus, while Derby were to face the part-timers from the Republic of Ireland, Finn Harps.

Finn Harps

Derby's start to the 1976/77 season had not been good, their only victory being a 2–1 win at lowly Doncaster Rovers in the League Cup a fortnight earlier. They came into the game on the back of two successive league defeats at Leeds United (2–0) and at home to Liverpool (3–2), leaving them in nineteenth place in the table. Their first three games of the season had ended as draws, but a worrying thing was that they had failed to score in three of the six games played so far.

15 September 1976
First round, first leg
Derby County 12–0 Finn Harps
Derby County: Moseley, Thomas, Nish, Rioch, McFarland, Todd (sub King 45 mins), Macken, Gemmill, Hector, George, James
Finn Harps: Murray, McDowell, Hutton, T. O'Doherty, Sheridan, Stephenson, D. O'Doherty (sub Logan 55 mins), Harking, Bradley (sub Mahon 63 mins), Healy, Carlyle
Referee: Mr Antoine Queudeville (Luxembourg)
Attendance: 13,353

During the close season Derby had lost Lee (retired), Hinton and Davies who were transferred to Dallas Tornado in the NASL and Club Brugge in Belgium respectively. None of these players had been replaced and there was a growing unease with the lack of transfer activity, although there were many factors involved. Boulton was no longer first-choice goalkeeper, being replaced by Graham Moseley.

The comments coming from the Finn Harps camp prior to the game indicated that they knew they would be in for a tough time and so had come to defend as much as possible. Dave Mackay held a lengthy team talk on the Monday afternoon engaging with his first team players and trying to ensure that they approached this game and Saturday's trip to Norwich City in the right frame of mind as they could not afford any slip-ups. As a reminder of this, on Tuesday Crusaders of Belfast (a similar standard to Finn Harps) were only just narrowly beaten by Liverpool in the European Cup.

Derby were attacking the Normanton End in the first half in front of Derby's lowest attendance for a European game – just 13,353. This low figure was probably due to the poor start to the season and the standard of opposition that Derby were playing. It was obvious from the start that the Irish team would be no match for Derby and by half time they had won the game and the tie and had the historians and statisticians checking the record books.

The first goal was timed at five minutes and two seconds; George passed the ball, taking the covering defender out of the game, to Hector on the edge of the penalty area and his shot was all along the ground and into the corner of the net. Gerry Murray in the Harps goal, probably the smallest goalkeeper in the League of Ireland,

The Finn Harps programme – one for the collectors – the club's record victory.

did not bother to dive for it. Unusually he did not kick the ball out once in the first half an hour, insisting on rolling it out to the nearest defender each time.

Goal 2 (11 minutes, 59 seconds). George collected the ball at the centre spot and drilled a through-ball that beat the defence giving Rioch the opportunity to shoot past the goalkeeper at his near post.

Goal 3 (19 minutes, 20 seconds). Gemmill's shot rebounded off a post out to Derby's left where James cut inside and shot, the ball taking a deflection off one of the eight defenders in the penalty area at that time.

Goal 4 (21 minutes, 39 seconds). A poor throw from the goalkeeper put Sheridan in all sorts of problems and he was robbed by Gemmill, who played it out wide to Rioch. Rioch's first-time cross was chested down by Hector who slipped the ball under Murray from four yards out.

Goal 5 (23 minutes, 59 seconds). Another poor throw from Murray was again intercepted by Gemmill on the right wing. His pass picked out George ten yards from goal and he swept it high into the net with ease.

Goal 6 (28 minutes, 1 second). A James cross was met by an unmarked George at the far post whose powerful header hit the underside of the bar and bounced down. His momentum carried him forwards and he headed a second time to make sure, while the goalkeeper was still rooted to the goal line.

Goal 7 (29 minutes, 2 seconds). Gemmill was involved again as he dispossessed the right-back and pushed the ball to James in the penalty area who cut inside the defender and curled a right-foot shot high into the corner of the net, past Murray who just stood and watched it.

Goal 8 (36 minutes, 30 seconds). Yet another roll-out by the goalkeeper towards the corner flag left the defender under pressure from Hector and the attempted back pass was intercepted by James who immediately laid it back for Hector on the edge of the area to place a shot from an acute angle into the far corner of the net, possibly with the aid of a deflection.

Goal 9 (38 minutes, 57 seconds). An indirect free kick inside the penalty area had Gemmill, Rioch and George standing over the ball. Tapped by Gemmill to George, his kick took a deflection off the shins of an onrushing defender and Murray wasn't able to hold onto the ball, it dropping nicely for Hector who had the whole goal to put it into.

Half time arrived with the score at 9–0 and Derby's place already booked in the next round. As always happens in these circumstances where one team so outclasses another, it is rare for the second half to yield as many goals. Todd was replaced at half time due to a slight strain and this allowed Macken to move into the back four and King to come into midfield.

Goal 10 (63 minutes, 24 seconds). A run by Rioch released Gemmill down the right wing and he squared the ball back to Hector who was able to turn and place the ball into the corner past a despairing dive.

Goal 11 (69 minutes, 10 seconds). Hector and King combined to set James running directly at the centre of the defence. As the defenders were closing in, he cut inside which wrongfooted the goalkeeper and calmly chipped the ball over a defender on the line to complete his hat-trick.

Goal 12 (75 minutes, 44 seconds). A rare foray into the Derby half was stopped by Macken on the edge of the penalty area. He passed to Gemmill in the middle of the Derby half all alone, who turned and immediately hit a left-foot pass to George ahead of the covering defenders and onside. He ran and shot from just inside the area to the keeper's right and into the corner to complete his hat trick.

The final scoreline of 12–0 set a new record for a Derby County score in a competitive game and was one short of the UEFA record (Cologne 13–0 Union Luxembourg in 1965). They could have scored more goals as there were at least five other occasions when shots hit the woodwork and Murray made some excellent saves in the second half. Finn Harps were a poor side and Derby went about the task very professionally showing their superior fitness, quality and skill. Hector scored five goals and became the seventh player in the club's history to score that number of goals in a game. He was also the first player to score five goals in a league game (Bradford Park Avenue v Barnsley, November 1965) and in Europe.

One consequence of there being twelve goals was that the 'Golden Goal' competiton had to pay out over £300 in prize money, barely breaking even on the night. The prizes on offer were £100 for the time of first goal and £10 for the time of any other goal. There were £2 prizes if your ticket was one second either side of the goal time and other random IOU winners.

29 September 1976
First round, second leg
Finn Harps 1–4 Derby County (Derby win 16–1 on aggregate)
Finn Harps: Murray, McDowall, Hutton, T. O'Doherty, J. Sheridan, Stevenson, Logan, Harkin, Bradley, Healy, Ferry
Derby County: Moseley, Thomas, Nish, Rioch, McFarland (sub Webster 16 mins), Todd, Newton, Gemmill (sub Macken 45 mins), Hector, George, James
Referee: Mr Jacques van Melkebeke (Belgium)
Attendance: 2,217

Derby still had not won in the league, having drawn the two games since the first leg and also earned a draw against Notts County in the League Cup. They were still in nineteenth place in the league and, approaching October, this was quite worrying.

Although the distance to the away match involved was not as far as some of the trips they had previously undertaken, it was certainly one of the longest. It took a five-and-a-half-hour coach journey from Dublin to the Londonderry border area. As the bus entered Ulster, the political situation at the time made it necessary for there to be armed British troops on the team bus. Finn Park is a cramped, non-league standard ground in the small town of Ballybofey in County Donegal.

Having such a huge goal difference from the first leg, it would have been tempting to make several changes to the usual Derby line-up. To Derby's credit they did send a full-strength squad which was appreciated by the officials of the home team, who ended up losing £800 over the two legs, having to cover their own expenses for the trip to Derby.

It would have been difficult for the Derby team to be motivated for this particular game as in reality all they had to do was play the 90 minutes to qualify, but they would be wary about not picking up any injuries. Derby gave the local fans something to cheer about within the first minute. A cross into the Derby area was headed down by

Todd to McFarland. McFarland tried to direct it back into Moseley's arm but put too much weight on it and managed to lob the ball over him and into the net for an own goal.

After sixteen minutes, McFarland was forced off with a hamstring strain and was replaced by Webster who took over at right-back with Thomas moving into the centre. This injury was to keep him out of the next two matches.

Despite taking the early lead, normality had been resumed by half time when Derby went into the break leading. After twenty-one minutes a firmly hit shot from Todd rebounded off the post and fell to Hector who side-footed the ball into the net from six yards. The same player was unlucky shortly afterwards when an excellent pass from Webster allowed him to shoot only for his strike to bounce off the crossbar.

Derby took the lead on thirty-two minutes when a James cross found Hector eight yards from goal and he had time and space to hold off the challenge from Sheridan, turn and slot it past Murray in goal. From now onwards it became more of an exhibition game, with neither team able to raise much enthusiasm for another forty-five minutes and Derby's passing and shooting not being accurate enough to pose any serious threat to the Finn Harps goal. Harps themselves hit the bar when Logan's long-range shot took a deflection off Nish's boot and had a couple of other shooting opportunities that ended up in the River Finn that flows behind one goal.

On eighty-one minutes Macken ran at the defence and pulled a number of defenders towards him. His square pass found George in lots of space and he had time to place his shot beyond the exposed goalkeeper. As the game moved into injury time, a firm shot from Rioch could not be held by Murray and it fell into the path of George who pushed it into the net.

A 4–1 win on the day gave an aggregate victory margin of 16–1 and, even though they did not play particularly well, the scoreline would have been by a wider margin but for the state of the pitch. It was described by Hector as, 'like playing on a sponge it was so soft underfoot.' The attendance of 2,217 was disappointing, especially for the home team, but in some ways inevitable given the score from the first leg.

AEK ATHENS

AEK had been playing in European competitions since 1963 without recording a win against any notable opposition until the first round of this year's competition when they beat Moscow Dynamo by a 3–2 aggregate score, scoring an extra-time goal in a 2–1 away defeat. They had six current Greek internationals in the squad, including a new signing, Mavros, who cost a Greek record fee of £240,000 from Panionios. They also had Dedes, the previous year's leading scorer in the league and other internationals purchased during the summer – Intzoglou (midfield), Nikloudis (midfield) and Christidid (goalkeeper).

20 October 1976
Second round, first leg
AEK Athens 2–0 Derby County
AEK Athens: Stergioudis, Tassos, Intzoglou, Ravousis, Nikolaou, Theodorides, Tsamis, Nikoloudis, Wagner, Papaioannou, Mavros
Derby County: Moseley, Thomas, Nish, Macken, McFarland, Todd, Powell, Gemmill (sub King 35 mins), Rioch, George, James
Referee: Mr F. Rion (Belgium)
Attendance: 35,000

Derby had beaten Notts County in the League Cup replay and had gained their first league win of the season at the weekend, inflicting a record defeat on Tottenham Hotspur by a score of 8–2 and climbing to eighteenth place. Rioch wore the number nine shirt and rewarded Dave Mackay by scoring four times. The fact they had to wait until mid-October for their win tells its own story.

The same team was selected to play in Athens, but a slight change of formation meant that Rioch was withdrawn into his usual midfield role, leaving James and George up front. There were two special plane-loads of fans that flew out to Greece from Heathrow for a total of £95, which included the coach fare to London.

The temperature in Athens would be well over 60 degrees and the players would have been made aware that the local crowd would be noisy and hostile to visitors; the information supplied to the club said 'the crowd has a poor reputation for sportsmanship.' The AEK manager thought that to get through the tie they would need to take a two-goal lead into the second leg in Derby in a fortnight, but he thought that they would have to play at their very best to get that result, while Dave Mackay was being defensive saying that Derby would have to be at their best to get anything from the game.

With thoughts of the last two European exits at Velež Mostar and Real Madrid, it was decided that a more defensive approach to the game should be adopted and to make the most of the home advantage. By playing a more defensive game, there would fewer chances created and the forwards would be expected to convert them. As expected there was a great deal of defending to be done in the early stages of the game and AEK were claiming a penalty in the opening minutes when a McFarland

ΣΤΑΔΙΟΝ
ΝΕΑΣ ΦΙΛΑΔΕΛΦΕΙΑΣ

The small programme for the AEK away game, one of the rarest Derby programmes.

clearance bounced and hit Gemmill on the hand. It was a case of ball to hand and not a deliberate hand ball so the referee was right in not awarding the spot kick. It is always dangerous to presume the actions of European referees and thoughts turned to the incident in Velež when a similar 'hand ball' was given that saw Derby eliminated.

Still in the early stages, a shot from Nikoloudis crashed against the underside of the bar and things from Derby's point of view died down. Having survived the early onslaught, Derby's players grew in confidence. Following the defensive tactics, they were happy to knock the ball along the back four and were prepared to bide their time before venturing forward. Rioch had the first of Derby's openings, firstly beating a couple of defenders before firing his shot wide and then, from further out, his firm shot curled and swerved forcing Stergioudis to push it round a post.

Derby's best opportunity of the first half came as a result of a free kick given when James was brought down by Ravousis when he had a clear run at goal. In modern football it was a sending-off offence, but on the day the defender was not even booked. Gemmill took the resulting free kick short to Nish, who freed Rioch on the left. Rioch's centre was driven low, but Thomas, on the far post, was unable to bundle the ball over the line – it was just at the wrong height to head, chest or shoot with accuracy. Having scored against Spurs at the weekend, it was too much to hope that the Welsh defender would score again so soon.

On thirty-five minutes, Gemmill went off with hamstring trouble and was replaced by King. A 0–0 scoreline at half time was very pleasing for Derby and they would hope to continue this; the longer the game remained scoreless, the more anxious and impatient the AEK players and fans would become. Derby's second clear opportunity came early in the second half when King and George exchanged passes that allowed King to square the ball back to George who tried to place his shot – hitting it with power first time may have yielded a better result. They were made to pay for these two missed opportunities by Wagner. On sixty-five minutes Papaioannou managed to get through a series of challenges on Derby's right and backheeled into the path of Walter Wagner, whose low, hard shot beat Moseley.

Just two minutes later Tassos got round Powell and ran along the goal line drawing the defence and goalkeeper towards him. He crossed the ball through everyone and left Wagner free to run in front of Rod Thomas to tap it into the net. Nikoloudis had a goal ruled out from a free kick and a header hit the bar.

For the last twenty-three minutes the AEK players seemed content with a 2–0 result and Derby regained some control after the two goals in three minutes. McFarland was Derby's best performer on the night, being dominant in the air and playing the ball well out of defence to Powell and Macken in the holding midfield roles. His display would ensure his inclusion in the England team to face Italy in a World Cup Qualifier in November.

In some ways the 2–0 defeat was a little unlucky as they had stuck to their plan throughout the game and if they had taken their chances before AEK had scored, the outcome could have been different. The programme for this game, nothing more than a teamsheet with the AEK logo on the front and printed on very thin yellow paper, is one of the rarest postwar Derby programmes, costing the equivalent of 8p, although there are stories of them being freely available only in the VIP areas. Only two have ever appeared for public sale.

Dave Mackay was pleased with the first hour when all appeared to be going to plan. He saw enough to suggest that when Derby attacked them at the Baseball Ground, the Greeks were going to find it tough to retain their composure.

3 November 1976
Second round, second leg
Derby County 2–3 AEK Athens (Derby lose 5–2 on aggregate)
Derby County: Moseley, Thomas (sub Macken 45 mins), Newton, Rioch, McFarland, Todd, Powell, Gemmill, Hector, George (sub Bourne 69 mins), James
AEK Athens: Stergioudis, Intzoglou, Theodorides, Ravousis, Nikolaou, Tassos, Tsamis (sub Papadopoulos 80 mins), Nikoloudis, Wagner, Papaioannou (sub Skerakis 59 mins), Mavros
Referee: Heinz Einbeck (East Germany)
Attendance: 28,746

The league continued to be a major concern – a defeat at Stoke City and a dull, uninspiring 2–0 victory over Bristol City left them in seventeenth place and sandwiched a draw at Third Division Brighton in the League Cup. Dave Mackay was

Programme for the last UEFA Cup tie at the Baseball Ground.

coming under increasing pressure to go and sign a new forward, although he had been trying to do that throughout the summer without success.

For this game season ticket holders were to use Cup Voucher 2 from their season ticket books, while all standing was to be by payment on the night of the game, costing 90p. Reports suggested that some 3,000 Greeks had flown in from Athens for the game and many more UK-resident Greeks were expected to attend.

Derby had never faced a two-goal deficit before and knew that they could not afford to give any goals away while at the same time having to score three times themselves. However, they also knew from the first leg that AEK were a useful team when attacking but were not so happy when being pressed back.

Papaioannou had a leg strain even before he started, but was such an important player for AEK it was felt he had to start the game. Likewise Archie Gemmill was not fully fit, but had to play for his energy and quality in the middle of the field.

From the start the Greek goalkeeper, Stergioudis, although appearing uncertain, was keeping everything that Derby threw at him out of the goal with a combination of luck and superb reflex saves. There were saves from George, James and importantly from Gemmill as half time approached when he was clean through. At the other end a free kick on twenty-four minutes found Papaioannou and his header came back off the bar with Moseley beaten.

Stergioudis was the hero of the first half as the game was scoreless at the break. This forced Derby to gamble for the second half with Macken replacing Thomas and playing with four forwards and three defenders. On fifty-three minutes Derby reduced the aggregate score when Gemmill and Rioch combined and Rioch's fired cross could not be held by the goalkeeper, the ball falling nicely to George to score. For a while Derby had AEK in trouble but two events on the seventy minute-mark sealed Derby's fate. Charlie George went off with a groin strain and immediately Powell fouled Wagner and Nikoloudis bent the free kick around the wall and past Moseley.

Nine minutes later Nikoloudis threaded a pass to Tassos whose shot went in off the post and, at 4–1 overall with ten minutes to play, the tie was over. A third AEK goal on eighty-five minutes followed when Powell's pass was intercepted and Wagner went round Moseley to score from an angle. Derby restored some respectability with two minutes left when Rioch turned in a Hector cross to make the score 3–2 on the night but it was still Derby's first home defeat in a European competition. AEK had played very well for an away team and deserved overall to progress to the next round. This was also one of Dave Mackay's last games in charge of the club as he was sacked before the end of the month, less than eighteen months after winning the League Championship title. AEK reached the semi-finals (having also beaten Queens Park Rangers along the way) where they were beaten by Juventus 5–1 over the two legs.

UEFA Cup 1976/77

First round
| 15 September 1976 | Derby County 12–0 Finn Harps | |
| 29 September 1976 | Finn Harps 1–4 Derby County | (W 16–1 on agg) |

Second round
| 20 October 2012 | AEK Athens 2–0 Derby County | |
| 3 November 2012 | Derby County 2–3 AEK Athens | (L 5–2 on agg) |

Anglo-Italian Cup 1992/93

The Anglo-Italian Cup originated in 1969 when Swindon Town won the League Cup, beating Arsenal in the final. Usually the League Cup winners would gain automatic entry into the UEFA Cup (or Fairs Cup as it was known then). Swindon Town, however, were refused entry on the grounds that they were a Third Division team at the time and so Arsenal took their place and went on to win the European trophy. To make things up to Swindon the Football League sanctioned an Anglo-Italian Cup Winners' Cup between Swindon Town and AS Roma that Swindon won. The joint attendance of over 54,000 and sponsorship by Esso meant that a full-blown tournament was organised.

However, by the mid-1970s the tournament had been demoted to non-league level and eventually disappeared altogether until 1992. With the formation of the Premier League, the Football League wished to promote and elevate the status of its own members and give them a taste of European football so decided to reintroduce the Anglo-Italian tournament, with the cooperation of the Italian FA.

The format of the competition was split into three distinct phases – a preliminary round where all the clubs in the newly-named First Division were split into eight groups of three teams, with each team playing each other once with one home game each. The winners of those eight groups were then to play an international stage in two groups against the eight Italian clubs entered into the competition. These games would all be against foreign opposition, two at home and two away. The results were compiled and the top English and Italian teams in each group went to a two-legged semi-final to create an English final and Italian final. The winners would meet in a grand final at Wembley Stadium.

The first preliminary round draw was made on a regional basis and put Derby in Group One along with Notts County (home) and Barnsley (away). The eight Italian teams competing included Bari, Cremonese and Ascoli all of whom had been relegated from Serie A the previous season. To ensure impartiality, for matches in England there would be an Italian referee and English linesmen, while the situation would be reversed for matches in Italy.

Notts County

Notts County

1862

2 September 1992
Preliminary round
Derby County 4–2 Notts County
Derby County: Sutton, Kavanagh, Forsyth, Pembridge,
Coleman, Wassall, McMinn (sub Gabbiadini 77 mins),
Kitson, T. Johnson, Williams, Simpson
Notts County: Catlin, Chris Short (sub Gallagher 86 mins),
Thomas, Craig Short (sub Walker 86 mins), M. Johnson, O'Riordan, Draper,
Turner, Wilson, Slawson, Smith
Referee: J.B. Worrall (Warrington)
Attendance: 6,767

Derby's season had not started well and they were still looking for their first win having suffered three defeats to newly promoted Peterborough United, Newcastle United and Leicester City, and they picked up a point in a goalless draw at Watford at the weekend – not a good start for the pre-season favourites for promotion. After four games without a win at the start of the season, there was an air of apprehension and nervousness going into the Notts County game. Passes were hurried and overhit as the players were trying their best, but things generally seemed to go against them.

They went from bad to worse after twenty minutes when Simon Coleman gave away a free kick on Derby's left. The free kick was met by Craig Short who powerfully headed past Steve Sutton. It wasn't until the forty minute-mark that Derby got on level terms when Paul Williams, who had not had a good start to the season, took a pass from Kitson and shot low past Catlin in the Notts County goal.

Three minutes later former Derby player Don O'Riordan pushed Tommy Johnson, and Mark Pembridge, in just his fifth game since his transfer from Luton Town in the summer, slammed in the resulting free kick for his second goal of the season. Before half time, there was another goal – the third in five minutes. Michael Forsyth gave away another needless free kick and Smith again took the kick, O'Riordan making no mistake with his header.

At the start of the second half, chances were created at both ends with Notts County having the better opportunities. Just on the hour, however, it was Derby who took the lead again when Williams put over a low centre that found its way to the far post where Simpson put it over the line.

Chances continued – Johnson headed over a McMinn cross when it was easier to score and McMinn was denied a penalty when brought down by Dean Thomas, while at the other end Wilson hit a post. McMinn did not last much longer as a deep cut on his knee meant that Gabbiadini replaced him and immediately used his physical strength against the defence. On eighty-five minutes he scored his first goal of the season after a Coleman free kick was flicked on by Kitson.

Arthur Cox, the Derby manager, said there was 'some very accurate, sharp and positive football.' Overall he was pleased with the display that gave Derby their first win of the season and they had started to convert a good percentage of the chances that had been created. On the other hand, he was not pleased with the number of unnecessary free kicks given away – especially as Notts County scored their goals from two of these. These defensive lapses needed to be addressed and within three weeks Cox had signed the Notts County centre-half, Craig Short, scorer of one of the goals, for a club record fee of £2.5m, which was also a British record for a defender. Unfortunately he would be ineligible for future games in the competition during this season having represented Notts County in the first game.

BARNSLEY

Derby had played at Barnsley in the league earlier in the month, forcing a 1–1 draw that kept Derby rooted to the bottom of the table. However, a first league win of the season against Southend United was sealed three days before this tie thanks to goals from Gabbiadini and Simpson.

29 September 1992
Preliminary round
Barnsley 1–2 Derby County
Barnsley: Butler; M. Robinson, J. Robinson, Bishop, Taggart, Burton, Liddell (sub Currie 72 mins), O'Connell, Rammell, Redfearn (sub Godfrey 88 mins), Archdeacon
Derby County: Sutton; Comyn, Forsyth, Coleman, Wassall, Pembridge, Johnson, Goulooze (sub Kavanagh 90 mins), Kitson, Gabbiadini (sub Hayward 88 mins), Simpson
Referee: Mr D.B. Allison (Lancaster)
Attendance: 3,960

Derby's new signings, Craig Short and Martin Kuhl, were unable to play in the competition as they had played for Notts County and Portsmouth respectively. Simon Coleman and another new signing, Richard Goulooze who had come from Dutch side SC Heerenveen, came into the team in their place. Paul Williams was not fit enough to play having been injured at West Ham United nine days earlier.

Derby's victory in the first game combined with the Notts County v Barnsley game ending in a 1–1 draw meant that Derby only needed to avoid defeat in this last game of the preliminary round to qualify as top of the group and move into the international stage where they would face four Italian teams. Barnsley had not won at home yet this season and the local fans were not enthused to come out so were outnumbered on the night by the travelling Rams fans, eager to taste European football again.

Paul Simpson, Mark Pembridge and Marco Gabbiadini were pulling the Barnsley defence around in the opening stages and it was no surprise that these three combined on seven minutes to put Derby in the lead. A Simpson cross was knocked down by Gabbiadini to Pembridge who curved a shot past Butler in the Barnsley goal. Pembridge had another shot well saved, Simpson went close with a chipped effort and Gabbiadini suffered a professional foul by Taggart when he broke clear of the defence. The referee only awarded a corner and gave a word of warning to the defender.

Barnsley were forced into a reshuffle to counteract the Derby attacks, withdrawing one of the forwards back into a midfield position. This gave them the opportunity to stifle the midfield area and the game became more even, although Steve Sutton was still largely a spectator and other than a set piece, there did not seem a way that the home team would score. Indeed, it was from a questionable free kick on Derby's left that they equalised on thirty-eight minutes. The free kick was sent over by Archdeacon and Taggart running across Sutton got the faintest of touches to glance it in.

Pembridge and Simpson were involved again for Derby's second goal on sixty-eight minutes. Goulooze started the move and a Pembridge pass found Simpson on the wing. His low centre missed Gabbiadini, but Kitson was at the far post to knock it back. Goulooze had kept running and was on hand to hit a low shot past Butler.

Pembridge was booked shortly afterwards when he badly fouled Redfearn, a result of many tangles between the two combative players throughout the game. This continued for the rest of the game and a further late tackle by Pembridge, unseen by the referee, eventually led to him being substituted. Goulooze picked up an injury and was replaced by Jason Kavanagh as the game entered an unprecedented six minutes of injury time.

It was a good night – Simon Coleman and Darren Wassall at the centre of the defence were in fine form and were responsible for giving Sutton a quiet night, while Goulooze's performance gave Arthur Cox another midfield option and the combination of Pembridge, Simpson and Gabbiadini was a handful for the opposition defence. Derby had done more than they needed to do and qualified for Europe for the first time since 1976/77 – the fans streaming away from the small, open terrace behind the goal were looking forward to seeing some Italian teams at home and on their travels.

The draw for the international stage was made on 2 October and Derby came out of the hat with Pisa, Cremonese, Reggiana and the most southerly club in the competition, Cosenza. Five of the top six teams in Serie B were competing in the Anglo-Italian competition – Cremonese were top, Reggiana second with Pisa and Bari a couple of points further behind. Derby had the best record of any of the English teams qualifying for the international stage, with their two wins and only Newcastle United matched Derby's six goals scored.

ASSOCIAZIONE CALCIO PISA 1909

11 November 1992
International group stage
Derby County 3–0 Pisa
Derby County: Sutton, Comyn, Forsyth, Coleman, Wassall, Pembridge, Johnson, Williams, McMinn, Gabbiadini, Simpson. Subs: M. Taylor, Micklewhite, Hayward, Kavanagh, Goulooze
Pisa: Ciucci, Chamot, Fasce, Fimognari, Lampugnani, Larsen, Rotella, Fiorentini (sub Gallaccio 45 mins), Scarafoni (sub Polidori 70 mins), Rocco, Vieri
Referee: Mr P. Fabricatore (Rome)
Attendance: 8,059

Derby had won four of their previous five league games, including wins at Luton Town, Wolverhampton Wanderers (2–0) and Notts County (2–0) and also had a creditable draw in the League Cup at home to Arsenal. However, they had just been beaten at home by Millwall (2–1). The home form so far this season was not great, having won only two and lost four games.

This was the first competitive European game in sixteen years, since the UEFA Cup defeat to AEK Athens in 1976. Ticket prices in all parts of the ground were reduced – by £1 for terraces and by £2 for a seat ticket (to £7). Arthur Cox was looking forward to the contrasting styles of football that would create interesting viewing and many talking points.

Pisa had just two foreign players remaining from their recent Serie A days – Argentinian defender José Chamot and Danish midfielder Henrik Larsen who was on loan from Serie A side Fiorentina and a target of Aston Villa. Larsen was in the Denmark team that won the European Championships in Sweden during the summer and was the leading scorer in that tournament. Also included in the team was Christian Vieri who has since been named in the FIFA 100, a list of the 125 greatest living footballers selected by Pelé as a part of FIFA's centenary celebrations. For a number of years he was regarded as one of the finest strikers in Europe, leading to him becoming the world's most expensive footballer in 1999 when Inter Milan paid Lazio £32 million for his services.

Pisa arrived at Birmingham airport on 10 November, training and staying at the Copthorne Hotel in Birmingham. For Derby, Paul Kitson was injured against Millwall and unfit so Tommy Johnson took his place while Simon Coleman and Paul Williams replaced Craig Short and Martin Kuhl who were ineligible. It wasn't long before Derby went in front (just eight minutes) when, after some good work from Forsyth, Simpson and Gabbiadini, Johnson was on hand to put the ball beyond the Italian keeper. Within two minutes the lead had been doubled when Andy Comyn's cross caused panic in the Italian defence and Johnson, Williams, Gabbiadini all tried to get the final touch. The ball eventually found its way to Forsyth to knock in his first goal of the season. Paul Simpson then missed a glorious opportunity from his favourite position when played in by Gabbiadini, but put his shot wide.

There had been a number of rough challenges throughout the game that resulted in bookings for Fiorentini, Fasce, Gabbiadini and Pembridge, and eventually a sending-off for the Pisa defender Chamot after he brought down McMinn from behind.

Vieri and Larsen showed only glimpses of their ability and even when presented with a one-on-one opportunity against Sutton, Vieri screwed his shot wide. The best goal of the night was reserved for the last minute when another Simpson corner could only be cleared to the edge of the area and Pembridge caught it perfectly to send his volley into the top corner. Arthur Cox said, 'we dominated the game tactically throughout. By subjecting them to conditions which they are not used to we enjoyed the cushion of a two-goal lead only ten minutes into the game.'

After the first round of games, the English clubs had won four of the eight games, two were draws and two defeats. Even at this early stage there were problems arising for the competition as a whole regarding low attendances, especially in Italy where the public had not shown much interest at all (the attendance at Derby was greater than the combined attendances at the four games played in Italy on the same night). The worst case was at Lucchese where just 733 attended the match against Newcastle United with half of them travelling from England.

COSENZA CALCIO 1914

24 November 1992
International group stage
Cosenza 0–3 Derby County
Cosenza: Graziani, Balleri, Marino, Napoli
(sub Losacco 56 mins), Bia, Gazzaneo, Monza
(sub Signorelli 36 mins), De Rosa, Negri, Fabris, Statuto
Derby County: Sutton, Comyn, Forsyth, Coleman, Wassall (sub Kavanagh 45 mins), Pembridge, Johnson, Williams, Kitson, Gabbiadini, McMinn
Referee: Mr A. Buksh (London)
Attendance: 4,263

There were two league matches since the Pisa game – an away win at Bristol Rovers (2–1) with goals from Johnson and Kitson and a home defeat to Sunderland (1–0). Conditions had been terrible with four hours of heavy rain before the start leaving standing water on the playing surface. Cosenza had missed promotion to Serie A by just one point the previous season and had won their latest game 2–0 at Verona leaving them fifth in the league table. Cosenza was not the easiest place to get to; the nearest airport was a commercial one at Lamezia, some 80km away. The official party of players and supporters flew out on the Sunday afternoon to Lamezia followed a ninety-minute coach journey up to Cosenza.

Derby would have over 150 fans in attendance with some travelling by train and others flying from Manchester to Naples and then getting the train or driving down to Cosenza. Even though it was late November, the weather was warm with temperatures into the '70s.

Travel itinerary for the Cosenza trip.

Paul Kitson heads Derby's second goal.

Derby were chasing their seventh successive away victory and as well as the enforced team changes through ineligibility, Paul Simpson was injured at the weekend and Ted McMinn came into the team. Roy McFarland said, 'obviously it is nice to be back in Europe; it's nice to be playing against a different style of football. It gives us a little bit of a deeper insight into our players and how they react in this kind of environment.'

Cosenza included a young Marco Negri in their team. Walter Smith paid £3.5m for him in his transfer from Perugia to Rangers in 1997, having scored 19 goals in 34 games for Cosenza. In 2004 had a trial with Derby but was not offered a contract.

Paul Williams was booked in the first few minutes when he made a two-footed challenge on a Cosenza player on the edge of his own penalty area. It wasn't long afterwards, however, that Derby took the lead. Ted McMinn was body-checked by the full-back the first time he tried get past him. The free kick was cleared for a corner and, as the Cosenza defence tried to play for offside, a punt from Pembridge found four Derby players onside, Comyn being the one to put the ball into the empty net.

Cosenza defender Balleri picked up a booking on ten minutes, inevitably for a foul on McMinn as the winger pushed the ball past him and was upended as he chased away. After eighteen minutes Derby extended their lead when good work from Pembridge out on the right wing led to a cross that Kitson headed past the goalkeeper from eight yards. Three minutes later the game was over as a contest when Williams picked up another poor clearance and chipped the ball over everyone for Gabbiadini to run onto and put a hard, low shot past the goalkeeper. A very high tackle from

Statuto on Wassall brought another booking for the Italians and also forced Wassall out of the game (and the next three), being replaced by Kavanagh at half time.

Having scored three goals in the first half, Derby did not have to do anything spectacular in the second half as Cosenza had shown little attacking threat before then – and nothing to suggest they could overturn a three-goal deficit. An extraordinary incident occurred just before the hour when Tommy Johnson was badly fouled in front of the dugouts. The player had already been booked and his team-mates surrounded the English referee, Alf Buksh, and among the generated confusion, he was booked for a second time – but without being sent off! The Derby bench could not believe it and the Italians very quickly substituted the offending player before the mistake could be rectified.

The second half passed relatively uneventfully with the Derby defence largely in command and restricting Cosenza only to long-range attempts at goal. Despite the constant niggly fouls and provocation from the Italian players, Arthur Cox's team were told to keep out of trouble and gave a very professional performance, especially the younger players in the squad. Cox commented, 'everything about our trip was very enjoyable and the hospitality extended to us throughout was first class, except, of course between 8.30 p.m. and 10.15 p.m. on Tuesday evening.'

Michael Forsyth, Derby's captain, said the second half was 'one of the most unpleasant forty-five minutes I have ever endured. The second half was horrible . . . provocation, body-checking, spitting.'

UNIONE SPORTIVA CREMONESE

8 December 1992
International group stage
Derby County 1–3 Cremonese
Derby County: Sutton, Goulooze (sub Kavanagh 17 mins), Forsyth, Coleman, Wassall, Pembridge, McMinn (sub Hayward 86 mins), Williams, Kitson, Gabbiadini, Simpson
Cremonese: Turci, Castagna, Pedroni, Cristiani (sub Piantoni 86 mins), Colonnese, Verdelli, Giandebiaggi, Ferraroni, Dezotti, Maspero, Florjancic (sub Pessotto, 72 mins)
Referee: Mr Walter Cinciripini (Ascoli)
Attendance: 7,050

Just two days before this game Derby had an away game at Swindon Town (live on TV) and came out 4–2 winners in torrential rain. That win set a new club record of six successive away wins in the league in a season (they had lost 2–1 at Arsenal in the League Cup during the week). The team showed three changes – as well as the cup-tied players McMinn came in for Johnson (injured during the Swindon victory) and Williams for Kuhl. Darren Wassall came in for his first game since the Cosenza game a fortnight earlier. These changes meant that the formation that worked so well at Swindon was changed to play with two wingers.

Cremonese were sitting top of Serie B, unbeaten after eleven games, and had a wealth of experienced players who had played in Serie A the previous season.

Derby were their own worst enemies after just five minutes when Steve Sutton failed to hold onto a relatively tame cross and spilt the ball in front of Florjancic, who tapped it into the net. Three minutes later they found themselves two goals down when another cross from Ferraroni caught Sutton in two minds and the ball came to Florjancic who tried to make an angle for a shot. Darren Wassall took the ball from him but only succeeded in putting it in the back of his own net.

Being two goals down was not ideal and on seventeen minutes, Richard Goulooze, playing at right-back, had to be substituted for Jason Kavanagh due to a strained hamstring. Within a minute Florjancic had scored again, with more sloppy defending to blame. Kavanagh only partially cleared the ball to Florjancic who ran past Wassall and Kavanagh and placed an excellent shot past Sutton from a tight angle.

Paul Simpson was having the best of the opportunities created at the other end, but found Turci in the Cremonese goal in top form. Three times he was able to turn away shots from the Derby midfielder to keep the score the same. Kitson, too, had shots saved before he got Derby back in the game on thirty-eight minutes. From a McMinn corner, Pembridge got in a shot that Kitson was able to intercept, turn and score from.

Derby's last real chances of the game came when Verdelli nearly directed a cross from Simpson into his own net and from another Simpson corner the same player clearly handled the ball when jumping with Paul Williams, seen by almost everyone apart from the referee who gave a free kick the other way for pushing. As for the second half, the Derby forward line could not find a way through the Cremonese defence and Brian Clough, watching from the Directors' Box, was offering advice to the Derby players without success.

Cremonese's performance was easily the best from an Italian team that Derby had faced during the competition so far and their comfortable win maintained their 100 per cent record and made sure they were the Italian qualifiers from Group B.

Manager Cox commented, 'We have only ourselves to blame. To give any side the sort of start we gave them with three goals in the opening twenty minutes of the game would offer problems for a comeback, but to do it against an Italian side that is used to grinding out 1–0 wins or goalless draws meant that we had given ourselves a mountain to climb.'

A place in the tournament semi-final (English final) place now rested on the following week's results, with Derby travelling to northern Italy to play Reggiana while the other contenders, West Ham United, were at home to Pisa. Derby had a superior goal difference (by three goals) and goals scored going into those games. Due to the time differences and kick-off time, West Ham would know what result they would require to progress before their kick-off, Derby kicking off at 7.00 p.m. local time (5.00 p.m. UK time).

ASSOCIAZIONE CALCIO REGGIANA 1919

For this crucial game there were two official tours on offer for fans; firstly, a coach trip costing £199, leaving Derby at 4.00 p.m. on Monday and arriving back in Derby in the early hours of Friday morning. Alternatively, there was an official flight with the team (allowing a maximum of 100 supporters) for £275 to Bologna, two nights in a hotel adjacent to the stadium and the package also included a day trip to the San Siro (correctly known as the Stadio Giuseppe Meazza) stadium and shops of central Milan.

The team departed on Monday lunchtime to Bologna and would leave immediately after the game, arriving back at 1.45 a.m. (UK time) on Thursday. On arrival, the temperature was -5°C and foggy. The foggy and misty conditions prevailing in and around the Po Valley during mid-December would linger throughout the entire stay and at one point it looked like the game would have to be put back twenty-four hours to give the weather a chance to clear or bring the kick-off forward to the afternoon.

The previous weekend's game saw a rare home victory for the Rams – 3–1 against Birmingham City, with goals from Johnson, Kitson and Williams.

16 December 1992
International group stage
Reggiana 0–3 Derby County
Reggiana: Bucci, Mozzini (sub Corrado 84 mins), Parlato, Monti, Dominissini, Accardi, Cherubini, Vivani, Pacione, Picasso, Sacchetti (sub Falco 73 mins)
Derby County: Taylor, Kavanagh, Forsyth, Comyn, Coleman, Pembridge, Johnson (sub Simpson 75 mins), Hayward, Kitson (sub Micklewhite 89 mins), Gabbiadini, McMinn
Referee: Mr D.J. Axcell (Southend)
Attendance: 598

Reggiana were the current leaders of Serie B with a three-point lead having beaten Cesena at the weekend. They made wholesale changes to their team – only four of the team which played in the league were in the team to face Derby. Derby had problems themselves; Sutton, Wassall and Goulooze were already ruled out, as was Paul Williams who had a stomach problem. Martin Taylor took over in goal for his first appearance in the competition and Andy Comyn came back into the first team while Steve Hayward was given his first start of the season.

Within three minutes of the start, a Johnson corner was not cleared and as the ball came back in from Hayward's header to Kitson, he beat the offside trap and had time to steer his shot past the goalkeeper. On twenty-eight minutes the lead was doubled when Hayward's forward pass to Gabbiadini was superbly controlled and knocked into space for Pembridge to strike his shot into the corner of the net for his tenth goal of the season. Hayward was again involved in the third goal before half time when his pass found Gabbiadini who went past his marker and around Bucci (who would be selected for the Italy World Cup squad in 1994) and rolled the ball in from a narrow angle.

Reggiana had plenty of possession but were unable to cause Derby any problems due to the well-marshalled defence denying them space and Taylor tidied up anything that did get through. Arthur Cox was pleased with the overall display – 'our football throughout the ninety minutes was very calculated and was interspersed with three excellent goals. Our attitude and approach to the fixture was very rewarding because, as I have said before, it is not easy to score goals and win games against Italian opposition.' There have not been many occasions when an English team has gone to Italy and won 3–0 and now Derby had done it twice in the same season.

West Ham knew what they had to do to overhaul Derby – the target was a 7–0 margin of victory but, surprisingly, they were held at home by Pisa. After the end of the international stage, Derby finished as the top English team in Group B. They were also top scorers at this stage with ten goals in the four games and attracted an average home attendance of over 7,500, beaten only by Newcastle United. Even at the semi-final stage of the resurrected tournament, the real concern lay with the extremely poor attendances for the games played in Italy. This point was enforced when the recent match at Reggiana (even though a midweek game in mid-December in the foggy conditions) attracted only 598, of which a couple of hundred had travelled from Derby. This attendance was in fact the lowest for a Derby County senior first team game in the twentieth century. The 598 was outdone though, when just 139 spectators turned up to the Lucchese v Birmingham City game that was played on the same night and Ascoli, who could have progressed to the semi-finals, mustered less than 500 for the visit of Portsmouth.

Another aspect of some concern was the disciplinary record – in the thirty-two games there were eighteen players sent off (nine from each country), but of those, sixteen were issued by Italian referees while in England.

BRENTFORD

Brentford were the only team in the competition to win all of their international stage matches with wins at Ascoli (3–1) and Cesena (1–0) and home wins against Lucchese (1–0) and Bari (2–1) – indeed, they had a 100 per cent record overall with qualifying round victories over Swindon Town and Oxford United. The sale during the previous summer of Dean Holdsworth to Wimbledon for £750,000 allowed them to go on a spending spree and fund several signings, including striker Joe Allon for £275,000 from Chelsea.

Derby had played Brentford at Griffin Park on Boxing Day, losing 2–1 and since then they had lost two more home league games (Portsmouth and West Ham), and had a goalless draw at Southend United and two FA Cup victories (2–1 against Stockport County and a 5–1 win at Luton Town four days earlier).

Programme for the first leg of the semi-final at Brentford.

27 January 1993
Semi-final, first leg (English final)
Brentford 3–4 Derby County
Brentford: Benstead, Bennett, Mortimer, Millen, Statham, Manuel, Allon,
Chalmers (sub Buckle 84 mins), Godfrey, Blissett, Luscombe (sub Gayle 84 mins)
Derby County: Sutton, Kavanagh, Forsyth, Coleman, Wassall, Pembridge,
Johnson, Comyn, Kitson, Gabbiadini, Patterson
Referee: A. Gunn (South Chailey)
Attendance: 5,227

After both teams topped their respective groups, they met in a two-legged semi-final,
the first leg being at Griffin Park where Derby had not won since 5 October 1946
(when they won 3–0). Derby had just played an FA Cup tie the previous Saturday,
away at Luton Town, which they had won 5–1, while Brentford were in league action
with a 1–0 defeat at Portsmouth, this being their fourth successive defeat. In terms of

league positions, there was just one point separating them, with Derby having the advantage.

As well as the cup-tied Short and Kuhl, injuries also ruled out Williams, McMinn and Goulooze from the midfield area. That meant a rare start for Mark Patterson who had last made an appearance at Barnsley in September and would have joined Preston North End if they had not sacked their manager halfway through the discussions.

Derby decided to play with three centre halves of Coleman, Wassall and Comyn to combat the physical forwards of Brentford while Derby's forward line of Gabbiadini, Johnson and Kitson had proved to be a match for any defence with their pace and movement. 750 Derby fans travelled to West London on a Tuesday night in January hoping to see a repeat of the other away fixtures in this competition and the semi-final followed the same pattern as the last away games in the competition (early goals) with Mark Patterson's shot into the corner of the net from the edge of the area on eight minutes after Tommy Johnson touched a Kitson cross into his path.

Ten minutes later Derby extended the lead when a long clearance by Steve Sutton reached Kitson, again in a wide position. His cross went over centre-half Bennett and came to Gabbiadini who had time to chest the ball down and shoot past keeper Benstead. The Rams were 3–0 up in the twenty-fifth minute when a long throw by Pembridge was not dealt with by the Brentford defence and Paul Kitson was left with an opportunity to score with some ease – his seventeenth goal of the season.

Once again Derby found themselves 3–0 up after thirty minutes and should have had the game well under control. This being the semi-final, though, Brentford were not going to give in as easily as the Italian opponents from previous rounds and the main threat was from free kicks or corners where they could target the physical presence of Allon and Blissett. On thirty-eight minutes, following a succession of corners, one was headed on by Blissett for Allon to head in at the far post, giving Brentford a lifeline. Just before half time, Allon scored his second goal and set up the second half as a thrilling encounter – Darren Wassall fouled Blissett, who took the free kick himself, a low and hard strike that Sutton could only parry into the path of Allon.

Tommy Johnson, could (and should) have put the game and tie beyond any doubt as three times he was put through by Pembridge. The first chance was deflected wide, Benstead came out well for the second to block him and the last hit the keeper's legs. Chances were also being created at an alarming rate at the other end despite the three centre-halves, with Allon and Luscombe both forcing saves from Sutton.

Derby gained some breathing space on seventy-five minutes when a Pembridge corner was not cleared by the home team and Patterson, following up, had one shot blocked but hit the rebound under the goalkeeper to give Derby a 4–2 lead. Steve Sutton was called upon on a regular basis but was eventually beaten with just five minutes remaining when Allon completed his hat-trick, heading in a Manuel free kick unchallenged. The Derby manager said it was 'a truly entertaining and exciting encounter,' while his Brentford counterpart revealed afterwards that, 'Joe Allon was rubbish in training yesterday – I just hope he will have a few more bad sessions.' As Gerald Mortimer commented, 'there were enough incidents and ingredients in the game to fill a book. Some of the defending was enough to turn managers grey overnight but there was deadly finishing from two teams flat-out for the final. The outcome was magnificent entertainment: no eye could stray for fear of missing another definitive moment. '

10 February 1993
Semi-final, second leg (English final)
Derby County 1–2 Brentford (5–5 on aggregate, Derby win on away goals)
Derby County: Sutton, Kavanagh, Forsyth, Coleman, Comyn, Pembridge, Johnson, McMinn (sub Williams 82 mins), Kitson, Gabbiadini (sub Mickelwhite 89 mins), Patterson
Brentford: Benstead, Statham, Mortimer, Millen, Bates, Manuel (sub Buckle 78 mins), Allon, Bennett, Godfrey, Blissett, Gayle (sub Luscombe 61 mins)
Referee: Mr K. Cooper (Pontypridd)
Attendance: 14,494

This was the first of six consecutive home games for Derby in various competitions having just completed four successive away games which they came through undefeated. The rules of the competition stated that extra time and penalties would be needed if the aggregate scores were level after ninety minutes, which meant only a 4–3 win in Brentford's favour would force the additional thirty minutes. Any other score would mean that away goals counted double in the event of the scores being level.

One milestone in the game was that referee Keith Cooper and the other officials were the first to wear purple shirts in a senior game – usually purple and yellow were reserve colours to be worn only on special occasions like cup finals and European games.

The game started at a brisk pace with Derby forcing early corners. Brentford's Godfrey was booked after just six minutes for a foul on Gabbiadini and received a lengthy lecture after fouling McMinn soon after. The bright start soon faded and both teams largely cancelled each other out, but with Brentford needing to win the game they showed little threat.

After forty-one minutes Derby took the lead when Pembridge pulled the ball back for Gabbiadini. His first touch was not good, but he followed up with a firmly hit shot that beat the goalkeeper and the men on the line. That put Derby 5–3 up with forty-five minutes to play and Brentford now having to score at least three times to win the tie. They almost pulled one back immediately when Patterson's back pass was intercepted by Gayle and his shot was turned away by Sutton's legs. At the other end Tommy Johnson smacked a shot against a post following a move that started with Steve Sutton then on to Kitson and Gabbiadini who set up the final shot.

On eighty-one minutes, Brentford equalised. A Forsyth header was not cleared and as the ball was played back in, Blissett hit a fine shot as he turned, the ball going in off a post. Just four minutes later Brentford took the lead on the night when Blissett scored again and squared the tie at 5–5, making for a nervous last few minutes. At the final whistle, no-one was sure whether extra time was to be played, but the referee had correctly called an end to the game and Derby had won through to their first Wembley appearance since 1975, courtesy of the away goals rule.

One unwanted statistic to come from the game was that it was the tenth home defeat of the season, probably the main reason why Derby were not challenging to escape from the First Division into the new Premier League.

Jason Kavanagh was booked but as a whole Derby had spread the bookings around the squad and as a result no-one would be suspended for the final. It had also been confirmed that the opponents at Wembley would be Cremonese who defeated Bari 6–3 on aggregate (a 4–1 win in the first leg and then a 2–2 draw) – more good news was that striker Florjancic failed to score for the first time in the competition although he remained the leading scorer.

27 March 1993
Final, Wembley Stadium
Derby County 1–3 Cremonese
Derby County: M. Taylor, Patterson, Forsyth, Nicholson, Coleman, Pembridge, Micklewhite, Goulooze (sub Hayward 83 mins), Kitson, Gabbiadini, Johnson (sub Simpson 81 mins)
Cremonese: Turci, Gualco, Pedroni, Cristiani, Colonnese, Verdelli, Giandebiaggi, Nicolini, Tentoni (sub Montorfano 85 mins), Maspero, Florjancic (sub Dezotti 73 mins)
Referee: Joaquín Urio Velasquez (Tolosa, Spain)
Attendance: 37,024

Wembley Stadium's capacity stood at 80,000 and Derby were allocated up to 60,000 tickets ranging in price from £11 to £26, so there was no issue in getting a ticket for anyone who wanted one. Derby's last appearance at Wembley was the Charity Shield in August 1975 and the stadium had changed little in the intervening eighteen years – the outside was still shabby, the seats uncomfortable and the view spoilt by the ring of posts going around the stands holding up the roof. No more than 1,000 Italians were expected to attend having made the 800-mile journey from northern Italy, although many London-based Italians would likely cheer on their team. The final was to be televised live on Italian station Rai Uno and with there being no Premier League games over the weekend, this was the biggest game in the country with only Glasgow Rangers attracting a bigger attendance in the UK.

Derby's recent league form was not good – three defeats (all 1–0) in their last four games left them lying in ninth place with a play-off place looking out of reach. Darren Wassall was out of the final with a fractured collarbone, but he said, 'they are the best team, not only that we came up against but, in the entire Italian side of the tournament . . . they'll be a tough challenge at Wembley.' The hero of the semi-final first leg, Mark Patterson, returned at right-back after missing the previous two games with a rib injury and Gabbiadini was under constant treatment to get him fit.

Cremonese were top of Serie B and were the bookmakers' pre-match favourites to take the trophy. They had a talented forward line of Slovenian Matjaz Florjancic (the leading scorer in the competition) and Andrea Tentoni (the current Serie B top scorer).

For many of Derby's players this was their first time playing at Wembley and for some the biggest game of their careers and a new experience. Gary Micklewhite had played in an FA Cup final for Queens Park Rangers and Paul Simpson with Oxford

Programme for the Wembley final against Cremonese.

United. Richard Goulooze was handed just his fourth start to make use of his passing ability on the wide Wembley pitch. With Kuhl cup-tied, the captaincy reverted back to Michael Forsyth who joined previous captains Jack Nicholas and Roy McFarland in leading out the Rams at Wembley.

Cremonese kicked off and immediately caused a number of problems with some dangerous probing runs from their dangerous front pair of Florjancic and Tentoni. After eleven minutes Cremonese took a deserved lead; Florjancic took a corner this time and curled the ball right under the bar where it was met by former Inter Milan defender Verdelli who bundled the ball past Taylor.

Derby had a couple of half-chances as Johnson shot into the side-netting and Coleman headed wide, but overall Derby were struggling to cope with the Italians.

The first booking came on eighteen minutes when Johnson, targeted as a possible dangerman, was fouled by Maspero. There was no doubt about the booking and the tackle left Johnson holding his knee in some discomfort. Five minutes later Derby equalised. Patterson picked the ball up and ran through the central midfield area before releasing Kitson on the left; his first-time cross was superbly headed by Gabbiadini into the goal, via a post.

Gary Micklewhite found a good position and was picked out by another Kitson cross. His shot was slightly mistimed and he hit it into the ground, taking all the power out of it. In what turned out to be an eventful first half, Cremonese were awarded a penalty on twenty-eight minutes when Forsyth made a bad tackle from behind on Giandebiaggi. There were no arguments about the decision and Nicolini hit his shot well into the corner. However, Martin Taylor joined a select few goalkeepers who had saved a penalty at Wembley Stadium to keep the scores level.

Chances continued to be created by the Italians, with Taylor stopping everything that was coming his way. At the other end there were only sporadic Derby attacks but despite the crosses being put over and free kicks given, they were unable to get a clear shot on target. The game had been a contrast of styles, as usual the continental players having better technique, vision and pace where Derby were relying on hard work, a rigid system and strength.

There was an early chance in the second half for Derby as Micklewhite's fine run found Gabbiadini and he was brought down just outside the penalty area. Pembridge took the free kick and he curled it just the wrong side of the post. A second penalty was awarded by the Spanish referee to Cremonese on fifty minutes as Tentoni got past Forsyth and fell over Martin Taylor as he came out to block the ball. Unlike the first penalty, this one was a debatable decision with the Derby players complaining bitterly. Maspero took responsibility this time and made sure the ball was out of the reach of the goalkeeper.

Gabbiadini was the most lively Derby forward, his bustling, physical style upsetting the stern Italian defence and there were some strong calls for a Derby penalty when Gualco seemed to foul him in the box. These two players finally had enough with each other and both were booked just before the hour mark following an off-the-ball incident and tangled again shortly afterwards.

Not all the bad challenges were from Cremonese – Shane Nicholson was lucky to escape with just a booking when he went in with a thigh-high challenge on Florjancic. With twenty minutes to go the game should have been all over as Florjancic broke the offside trap and although he had Giandebiaggi up in support and unmarked in the centre of the goal, he decided to take the shot himself and put the ball into the side-netting. Shortly afterwards Tentoni pulled the ball back for Nicolini and beat Taylor with his shot but the ball hit the post and bounced away to safety.

Dezotti was brought on to replace Flojancic – Dezotti was the top scorer last season and gained 'fame' in the 1990 World Cup final when he became the second of the Argentinians to be sent off in the game against Germany. As one reporter said at the time, bringing him on 'was akin to hosing down a blaze with gasoline.'

Some of the Italians' antics and professional and personal attacks were getting too much, with Kitson being stamped on in full view of the referee. Pembridge didn't fare any better, being punched while offering to help up Dezotti. His punch left

Pembridge with a mark underneath his left eye for a number of days afterwards, but Dezotti was not booked.

Eventually, after eighty-three minutes and with Derby tiring, Cremonese got the third goal they deserved when the impressive Tentoni chased a through-ball, beat Forsyth for pace and shot under Taylor from an angle. Arthur Cox admitted that, 'Their quality was too much for what we had. Over ninety minutes we can have no complaints about the result but it was a major disappointment to us as we did not do ourselves justice.' With over 36,000 Derby fans inside Wembley, Chairman Brian Fearn said 'our fans were magnificent but we were beaten by a better team.'

Cremonese's main objective of the 1992/93 season was to secure promotion to Serie A which was achieved and the following season they finished a respectable tenth position. The 'international stage', as it was officially described by the League, had produced eighty goals, seventy-nine bookings and eighteen sendings off in the thirty-two matches, but attendances in Italy had been poor and with all the costs of air fares and hotels, Derby had to reach the final to stand a chance of making any profit. It also contributed to Derby's busiest ever season – the nine matches leading up to the final were alongside a forty-six-match league campaign and reaching the FA Cup sixth round (five matches) and League Cup third round (four matches), which resulted in a total of sixty-four matches, beating the previous club record of sixty from the 1985/86 season.

Anglo-Italian Cup 1992/93

Preliminary round

2 September 1992	Derby County 4–2 Notts County
29 September 1992	Barnsley 1–2 Derby County

International Group Stage

11 November 1992	Derby County 3–0 Pisa 1909
24 November 1992	Cosenza 0–3 Derby County
8 December 1992	Derby County 1–3 Cremonese
16 December 1992	Reggiana 0–3 Derby County

Semi-final (English final)

27 January 1993	Brentford 3–4 Derby County
10 February 1993	Derby County 1–2 Brentford
	(5–5 on aggregate, Derby win on away goals)

Final

27 March 1993	Derby County 1–3 Cremonese

Anglo-Italian Cup 1993/94

The previous season Derby had played nine matches in the competition in reaching the final which added to the already-crowded fixture list and in so doing set a club record of sixty-four senior games in a season. As previously mentioned, financially it was not good for the clubs and the only way Derby made a profit was by reaching the final. With the two- or three-day trips to Italy being the main costs and with West Ham United making a £40,000 loss on their games, the long-term viability of the competition was unsustainable without a rethink from the organisers.

The League tried to make attractive local derbies for the preliminary first round and boost the attendances in the poorly supported tournament. Group Two had Derby, Notts County and the newly relegated Nottingham Forest – the only time that the East Midlands derby games have taken place in a European competition. The format of the competition remained unchanged with the eight group winners moving forward to play the eight Italian teams. In the first round of the competition it is almost impossible to qualify to the international stage if a club gets beaten and there is a definite advantage in playing in the last game of the round as both teams would know exactly what result either team would require to progress.

The eight Italian teams taking part in this year's competition would be Fiorentina (coached by Claudio Ranieri and with strikers Batistuta and Francesco Baiano, who was to join Derby several years later), Ancona, Brescia and Pescara all relegated from Serie A, as well as Ascoli, Pisa, Padova and Cosenza. The previous season's winners, Cremonese, had been promoted to Serie A at the end of the season along with Reggiana, soundly beaten 3–0 by Derby, as champions.

Summer moves in the transfer market saw Patterson, Comyn, McMinn and Micklewhite depart, replaced by right-back Gary Charles from Nottingham Forest for a fee of £750,000 and USA international John Harkes from Sheffield Wednesday.

Notts County

Notts County

1862

31 August 1993
Qualifying round
Notts County 3–2 Derby County
Notts County: Cherry, Wilson, M. Johnson, Chris
Short, M. Simpson, Walker, Devlin, Dijkstra, Lund,
Slawson, Legg
Derby County: Taylor, Charles, Forsyth, Kuhl, Craig
Short, Wassall, Harkes, Pembridge, Kitson, T. Johnson,
P. Simpson
Referee: Mr K.P.J. Barratt (Coventry)
Attendance: 3,276

Tommy Johnson, making a return to his former club, started for the first time that season, replacing Gabbiadini. Pembridge moved into a central midfield position to take over from Williams and Simpson played out on the left wing.

In the first few minutes both teams had headers rebound off the bar – Michael Johnson for Notts County and Short for Derby. Notts County took the lead after just seven minutes when Charles tried to let a ball roll out of play for a goal kick and was robbed by Slawson who pulled the ball back for Andy Legg to shoot past Taylor. Derby's forwards were largely anonymous during the first half and failed to trouble Steve Cherry in the Notts County goal.

Immediately after the restart the scores were levelled when Tommy Johnson laid the ball back to John Harkes to shoot into the corner for his first goal for Derby since his summer move. The scores were level for less than two minutes, however – the Notts County secret weapon was Legg's long throw which caused a constant problem whenever they were near the penalty area; from one of these Slawson flicked on for Lund to head past Taylor.

Derby then had their best spell of the game when they created several good chances – Pembridge, Short, Kitson and Johnson all had shots blocked, saved or lost control at the crucial time. After all the chances came and went, it was Notts County that went further ahead on sixty-nine minutes when a cross from Dijkstra picked out Legg who was all alone and dived to head in. Tommy Johnson made the score 3–2 with six minutes left when he was on the end of a Kuhl cross that was turned on by Simpson.

Defensive mistakes were responsible for all three goals and ultimately lost this game for Derby; they scored two goals and could, with greater composure, have scored two or three more and should have taken something from the game. Martin Kuhl was the pick of the Derby players, but they missed the energy and drive of Williams.

NOTTINGHAM FOREST

8 September 1993
Qualifying round
Derby County 3–2 Nottingham Forest
Derby County: Taylor, Charles, Forsyth, Kuhl, Short, Wassall, Johnson, Williams, Kitson, Gabbiadini, Simpson
Nottingham Forest: Crossley, Lyttle, Laws, Blatherwick, Chettle, Stone, Gemmill, Glover (sub McGregor 85 mins), Rosario, Collymore, Woan
Referee: Mr V.G. Callow (Solihull)
Attendance: 6,654

Having lost the first game, Derby came into this match knowing that anything other than a victory would mean an early exit from the competition. Ideally, Derby wanted a comfortable win scoring a number of goals in the process and in the last match of the group, a narrow win for Forest would see Derby qualify.

Arthur Cox, although still manager in name, was unable to work during this time due to a back injury and Roy McFarland and the rest of the coaching staff were running the club on a day-to-day basis, with Cox having to review things from his home. This back injury was to remain with Cox and within a month he felt he had to resign as manager, with McFarland taking permanent charge.

Forest had been relegated from the new Premier League at the end of the previous season, a season which also saw Brian Clough retire as manager to be replaced by Frank Clark. Relegation meant that Roy Keane joined Manchester United for a British record fee of £3.75m while Nigel Clough went to Liverpool and Gary Charles to Derby. International call-ups also left them without Stuart Pearce, David Phillips and Kingsley Black. Stan Collymore was in line to make his first full appearance following his £2.2m move from Southend United.

The teams had met already that season at the City Ground (the second match of the league season), where they fought out a 1–1 draw with Forsyth scoring for the

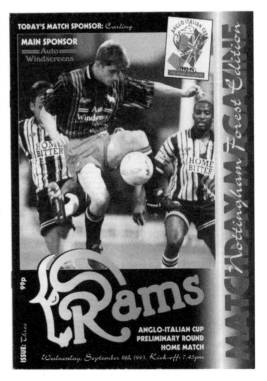

Programme for the visit of Nottingham Forest in the preliminary round.

Rams. Derby's two home league matches so far had both finished in wins (5–0 v Sunderland and 1–0 v Bristol City). The away form was not so great, however, with just a draw to show from four matches, including a 3–0 reverse at Birmingham City the previous weekend in what was a very poor Derby performance. There were two changes from that game, Wassall being replaced by Coleman and Johnson in for Harkes who had picked up a knee injury.

There was torrential rain before kick-off, which had an effect on the attendance figure, and standing water in the middle of the pitch made passing in that area very difficult. As usual for a local derby game, there were some rough tackles early on in the game and Kuhl, Laws, Williams and Rosario soon found themselves in the referee's notebook.

The best of the chances went to the visitors, one gifted to them by Charles whose attempted pass across the defensive line was intercepted, although Stone could not take advantage. Most of Derby's chances fell to Gabbiadini, but twice he shot wide when set up by Williams and Kitson. Just after half time the visitors took the lead when a Glover shot skidded off the surface and over Taylor. For the next twenty minutes Forest dominated, going further ahead when Short tried to be too clever and only succeeded in passing the ball to Scott Gemmill who scored easily. Woan, Rosario and Glover all had decent chances to put the game beyond Derby and Taylor had to be at his best to keep them out.

On sixty-seven minutes, Derby got a lifeline when a free kick was well worked by Johnson and Kuhl to set up Simpson to curl a low shot into the corner for his first goal of the season. Kitson equalised just two minutes later when he pounced on the ball just as Williams was turning to shoot at goal himself. The game looked to be heading for a draw, and elmination for Derby, until three minutes from the end when Simpson's corner was only cleared to Kuhl who shot hard and low and Des Lyttle's attempted clearance on the goal line only saw the ball divert into the opposite side of the net.

With both matches finishing with a 3–2 score to the home team, there was just one game left to play (Nottingham Forest v Notts County) to decide the group winner. One result would still be possible that would cause everyone to reach for the rule book – a 3–2 win for Forest. In that eventuality, lots would have to be drawn to determine the group winner. However, that was unnecessary as a week later the two Nottingham clubs played out a 1–1 draw which was enough for Notts County to progress to the international stage of the competition, while Forest finished bottom of the group. They were joined by the other group winners – Middlesbrough, Bolton Wanderers, Southend United, West Bromwich Albion, Stoke City, Charlton Athletic and Portsmouth.

ANGLO-ITALIAN CUP 1993/94

Qualifying round

31 August 1993	Notts County 3–2 Derby County
8 September 1993	Derby County 3–2 Nottingham Forest

Anglo-Italian Cup 1994/95

This was the third season of the resurrected competition and again the structure of it was changed, an indication from the organisers that the competition was not working in its current format. The invitation to take part was based on league positions – the five highest non-promoted teams plus the three relegated from the Premier League. Oldham Athletic and Millwall declined and their places were taken by Middlesbrough and Stoke City.

For this season, the preliminary English groups were dispensed with and the competition started with the international stage. Derby were drawn in Group B along with Middlesbrough, Sheffield United and Stoke City and would play against four Italian teams (Ancona, Cesena, Piacenza and Udinese), two at home and two in Italy.

Associazione Calcio Ancona

24 August 1994
Inernational stage
Ancona 2–1 Derby County
Ancona: Pinna, Nicola, Sergio, Sgro, Baroni, Germoni
(sub Cornacchia 45 mins), Baglieri (sub Cangini 72 mins),
De Angelis, Caccia, Catanese, Centofanti
Derby County: Taylor, Charles, Forsyth, Kuhl, Nicholson
(sub Kavanagh 74 mins), Wassall, Stallard, Hayward
(sub Cowans 74 mins), Gabbiadini, Pembridge, Simpson
Referee: Mr P.L. Foakes (Clacton-on-Sea)
Attendance: 748

Derby had just picked up their first point of the season with a 0–0 home draw against
Luton Town, having lost the opening game 2–1 at Barnsley. For the game in Italy there
were a number of enforced team changes with Johnson, Williams, Harkes, Short and
Sturridge all missing, while Cowans was rested.

It was the forward line that was giving the most cause for concern; with Johnson and
Sturridge already injured and with Gabbiadini about to start a three-match ban, Roy
McFarland did not want to risk his only other forward, Paul Kitson, getting injured.
All of those changes meant that Kuhl and Stallard would start a game for the first
time that season. With only one forward, it was the responsibility of the midfielders
to get upfield as often as possible in support. The new formation was working well
and after good work from Kuhl and Hayward, Charles sent over a perfect cross for
Pembridge to dive in and bury his header. Derby were in control until the thirty-fifth
minute when Gabbiadini lost the ball and a typically quick Italian counter-attack
found Caccia free to send Forsyth the wrong way before placing a shot wide of Taylor.

Another defensive error just before half time saw the home side take the lead
as Forsyth and Simpson failed to clear the ball out of the penalty area, allowing
Caccia to score with a fierce shot. There were half-chances for Derby to draw level
in the second half, the majority of them requiring a player to take a strike at goal
instead of having an extra touch or pass. Once Cowans was introduced in place
of Hayward, Derby pushed further forward and Kavanagh hit the outside of a post,
while Gabbiadini shot narrowly wide on a return pass from Stallard. For all that,
Ancona, who had replaced their sweeper with an additional midfield player at half
time, looked comfortable once they had the lead. The attendance of just 748 in a
new stadium that was built for Ancona's brief stay in Serie A three years earlier did
not make for a good atmosphere.

Roy McFarland said, 'we gave away two very poor goals, the second coming
right on the stroke of half time, having opened the scoring ourselves with a classic,
counter-attack move. In the second half we dominated play and were unlucky not to
get something out of the game.'

ASSOCIAZIONE CALCIO CESENA

After the first round of matches, only Stoke City and Wolverhampton Wanderers recorded victories for the English league, both winning in Italy. Stoke had won 2–0 at Derby's next opponents, Cesena.

6 September 1994
Inernational stage
Derby County 6–1 AC Cesena
Derby County: Taylor, Charles (sub Kavanagh 45 mins), Nicholson, Hodge, Short, Wassall, Cowans, Carsley, Kitson, Gabbiadini (sub Sturridge 25 mins), Simpson
AC Cesena: Santarelli, Scugugia, Calcaterra, Ambrosini, Aloisi, Sussi, Teodorani, Del Bianco (sub Piangerelli 45 mins), Zagati (sub Maenza 45 mins), Piraccini, Hübner
Referee: Mr Libero Brignoccoli (Ancona)
Attendance: 2,010

After four defeats and a draw, Derby finally got a win at the weekend with a 2–1 home victory over Grimsby Town, leaving them in twenty-first position in the league table after five games. For the second successive match in the competition, Derby were without several key players. Harkes and Pembridge were away on international duty (USA and Wales respectively), Williams and Johnson were still injured and Forsyth was not risked. Steve Hodge had arrived from Leeds United on loan and Lee Carsley was given his debut even though he had played for and scored twice for the reserves the night before.

Cesena should have scored early on when a superb pass inside the full-back put Del Bianco in on goal, but Taylor raced out to block the shot. As Alan Hinton used to confuse and deceive foreign goalkeepers in the 1970s, so Paul Simpson began to do so against Santarelli in the Cesena goal. Derby's first goal came on eight minutes when a Charles cross was only headed out to Hodge, who had time to control the ball before volleying low past the keeper. After that Simpson began to put lots of crosses over, and goals followed.

On sixteen minutes Simpson collected a Nicholson clearance and his excellent cross was met by Kitson who nodded the ball into the net. Gabbiadini had to go off with a twisted knee but it did little to upset Derby's attacks. A Simpson corner on twenty-eight minutes was headed on by Short and Kitson was able to get to the ball first and score. Three minutes later another Simpson corner was flicked on by Sturridge and another Kitson header made the score 4–0, a first career hat-trick for the striker.

Another Simpson cross caught the goalkeeper in two minds and that left Hodge to score his second goal of the night with yet another header. Charles had been struggling with a thigh injury and was substituted at half time with the game won. As Derby sat back on the lead Cesena had a couple of chances, one deflected free kick hitting a post and another chance smacking against the bar.

Kitson bagged his fourth goal on seventy-one minutes resulting from another Simpson cross that eventually went in off the post. Cesena finally scored on seventy-nine minutes when a cross from the left found its way to Ambrosini to finish with a simple header. After this they had further opportunities to narrow the scoreline, but two superb saves from Taylor kept them out.

PIACENZA CALCIO

Derby's results had improved over the last month, losing just one of the five league games which had seen them rise to ninth place and progress to the next round of the League Cup after defeating Reading over two legs.

5 October 1994
International stage
Piacenza 1–1 Derby County
Piacenza: Ramon, Di Cintio, Manganiello (sub Moretti 50 mins), Suppa, Cesari, Lucci, Turrini, Brioschi, De Vitis, Iacobelli, Piovani
Derby County: Sutton, Charles, Nicholson (sub Kavanagh 45 mins), Carsley (sub Davies 76 mins), Wassall, Williams, Cowans, Sturridge, Harkes, Pembridge, Simpson
Referee: Mr J. Lloyd (Wrexham)
Attendance: 1,710

Derby's squad was stretched again for this game, with Gabbiadini, Johnson, Short, Hodge, Forsyth and Taylor all unavailable. Martin Taylor picked up a shoulder injury during the defeat at Bolton at the weekend bringing an end to his sequence of ninety-three consecutive appearances. These changes meant that Sturridge would have to play as the only striker and be supported with a midfield five of Carsley, Cowans, Harkes, Pembridge and Simpson.

Piacenza had drawn four out of their five Serie B league matches and both of the Anglo-Italian games they had played, so a betting man would go for a draw as the result. The first half was a largely forgettable affair with only one chance of note for either team, Derby's coming from Simpson whose volley was tipped over the bar by the home goalkeeper.

It wasn't until just after the hour mark that the game livened up; Brioschi went over in the penalty area without being touched, the referee assuming either that Wassall had tripped him or that he had been pulled back by Harkes. Either way, a penalty was given which De Vitis scored.

Thirteen minutes from the end, Derby equalised when a corner from Simpson was headed on by Wassall, the ball falling nicely for Williams to volley into the net. Williams was the star of the show and the goal capped an excellent performance from the centre-half.

Derby gave a debut to another homegrown player when Will Davies replaced Carsley. With nine minutes left, Pembridge had the perfect chance to win the game when a Simpson corner came over and Turrini elbowed Wassall in the face, the referee sending off the home player and awarding a penalty kick. Pembridge took the penalty and saw it parried by Ramon in goal (his first penalty failure for Derby) and then slid in to force the ball and goalkeeper over the line that started a melee under the crossbar. The referee, who had lost complete control of the game by this stage and had already booked fourteen players, gave the home side a free kick.

A 1–1 draw was a good result given the number of players that were missing and that the young players in Sturridge, Carsley and Davies played a substantial part in the game. However, they should have won, especially as Stoke managed to get an impressive 3–1 win at Udinese and that put them three points ahead of Derby with one game of this initial stage to play. Derby had to beat Udinese and hope that Stoke were beaten at home by Piacenza on the same evening to go through to the semi-finals.

UDINESE CALCIO

15 November 1994
International stage
Derby County 3–1 Udinese
Derby County: Sutton, Charles (sub Kavanagh 76 mins),
Nicholson, Kuhl, Short, Williams, Harkes, Carsley,
T. Johnson (sub Cooper 85 mins), Stallard, Sturridge
Udinese: Battistini, Compagnon, Bertotto, Pierini, Calori,
Ripa, Lasalandra, Scarchilli, Benchelli (sub Prevedini 82 mins), Pizzi, Poggi
Referee: Mr Franceschini (Bari)
Attendance: 1,562

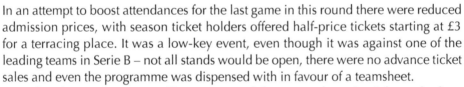

In an attempt to boost attendances for the last game in this round there were reduced admission prices, with season ticket holders offered half-price tickets starting at £3 for a terracing place. It was a low-key event, even though it was against one of the leading teams in Serie B – not all stands would be open, there were no advance ticket sales and even the programme was dispensed with in favour of a teamsheet.

Derby's league form was still not great and they were down in eighteenth place following a run of just two wins in the previous ten games, one of which was a League Cup victory at Portsmouth. There were five changes to the team that was defeated at Sheffield United at the weekend – Forsyth, Gabbiadini, Cowans and Simpson were missing but Short was available again after recovering from 'flu. Udinese also had to win the game and rely on Ancona failing to beat Middlesbrough to reach the semi-finals in Italy.

With their current form and having to win this game to stand any chance of getting any further in the competition, Derby began nervously and Sutton, now in charge of the goalkeeper's jersey since Martin Taylor's horrific leg-break at Southend, had to be alert a number of times in the early stages.

Sloppy defending from the Italians on eighteen minutes gifted the first goal when a routine cross from Nicholson made Bertotto and Calori stop and wait for each other to clear the ball – neither did and Johnson scored. Almost immediately, the lead was doubled when Kuhl played a pass to Stallard who forced his way between two defenders before drawing out the goalkeeper and clipping the ball over him. More opportunities came before half time as Sturridge shot wide and Carsley's volley was pushed away by Battistini.

A mistake by Charles early in the second half allowed Bertotto to score and they also hit a post when the home defence lost their bearings – it looked at this stage that Udinese would get an equaliser and possibly go on to win the game. Derby got the decisive goal however, on seventy minutes, when Williams headed on a corner at the near post for Johnson to rattle in a shot. Just after that Charles suffered a hamstring injury and was replaced by Kavanagh and potentially brought an end to the transfer speculation linking Charles with a move to Leicester City.

Kevin Cooper came on for the last five minutes in place of Johnson and became the third youngster to make his debut in the competition that season, following Carsley and Davies.

The attendance for the game, despite the low prices, was poor and was the lowest for a senior competitive game at the Baseball Ground for nearly 100 years. With this sort of statistic, even for a well-supported club like Derby, there could be little future for the competition. Stoke City only needed a draw to qualify but comfortably beat Piacenza 4–0 so went through to the two-legged English final against Notts County.

ANGLO-ITALIAN CUP 1994/95

International Stage
24 August 1994	Ancona 2–1 Derby County
6 September 1994	Derby County 6–1 AC Cesena
5 October 1994	Piacenza 1–1 Derby County
15 November 1994	Derby County 3–1 Udinese

Missed Out

As well as the years when they qualified and took part in the official competitions, there were also several years when Derby County were denied the opportunity or chose not to participate in Europe.

INTER-CITIES FAIRS CUP 1962/63

In a board meeting in June 1962 the directors decided not to apply for entry to this European competition which was set up to promote international trade fairs. The competition was initially only open to teams from cities that hosted trade fairs and where these teams finished in their national league had no relevance. This was a competition that was not organised by UEFA and as such records of the competing clubs are not included in any UEFA European club statistics.

INTER-CITIES FAIRS CUP 1970/71

Top Ten in Division One, 1969/70

Team	P	W	D	L	F	A	W	D	L	F	A	Pts
Everton	42	17	3	1	46	19	12	5	4	26	15	66
Leeds United	42	15	4	2	50	19	6	11	4	34	30	57
Chelsea	42	13	7	1	36	18	8	6	7	34	32	55
Derby County	42	15	3	3	45	14	7	6	8	19	23	53
Liverpool	42	10	7	4	34	20	10	4	7	31	22	51
Coventry City	42	9	6	6	35	28	10	5	6	23	20	49
Newcastle United	42	14	2	5	42	16	3	11	7	15	19	47
Manchester United	42	8	9	4	37	27	6	8	7	29	34	45
Stoke City	42	10	7	4	31	23	5	8	8	25	29	45
Manchester City	42	8	6	7	25	22	8	5	8	30	26	43

Derby had finished fourth in the league, the fifty-three points they had gained equalling their best ever in the division and it was their highest finish for over twenty years. The building of the modern Ley Stand increased the seating capacity and fans were purchasing season tickets for a couple of years at a time – money was flowing into the club. For some time the financial books and records of the club had been in the hands of a joint Football Association and Football League commission and they found a number of issues during their investigations which were raised when they announced their findings:

1) the 1969 financial accounts had showed there was a shortage of £3,000 from the season ticket receipts

2) there were discrepancies in the way that lodging fees were being paid to various landladies

3) some player contracts were not correctly lodged with the relevant football authorities

4) £2,000 was paid to captain Dave Mackay for his programme notes during the season which was outside the terms of his contract placed with the Football League

The result was that Derby were found guilty of gross negligence in their administration of the club and fined a total of £10,000 for financial irregularities that implicated Brian Clough, with Derby secretary Stuart Webb claiming that, 'Clough was running round with bins full of cash . . . one disappeared' (Mail Online by Ian Ladyman, 25 March 2009).

The fine of £10,000 was a record fine for a club and that was made worse as they were also banned from all European competitions for a year, meaning that they were to lose out on their place in the Fairs Cup. Although those punishments were bad enough, it could have been much worse as automatic relegation was one of the options open to the Commission and indeed Swindon Town suffered that fate in the 1990s when they were denied promotion to Division One for similar contractual irregularities.

Paying the fine was not a problem to the club, but it was the fans and players who missed this opportunity to match themselves against some of the best teams in Europe. The likes of Willie Carlin, Les Green and particularly Dave Mackay (who was entering his last year as a Derby player and whose experience would have been invaluable) would leave Derby during the 1970/71 season and never play for the club in Europe. Some of the potential opponents in the Fairs Cup were Athletic Bilbao, Barcelona, Bayern Munich, Inter Milan, Juventus, Lazio and Glasgow Rangers. Derby's place went to Newcastle United, who were drawn against Inter Milan in the first round.

As they were unable to play in European competitions, the ban also included entry from the new Texaco Cup tournament, which was classed as an international tournament as it involved teams from Scotland and Ireland. Pre-season matches in France and Germany were also cancelled and the team instead took part in football's first sponsored competition, the Watney Cup, which they won by beating Manchester United 4–1 in the final at the Baseball Ground. The fine was agreed to be paid at a board meeting held on 13 August 1970.

Anglo-Italian Cup 1971/72

Luigi Peronace, who was instrumental in the organisation of the competition in the first place, had invited Derby to enter the competition as part of the pre-season build-up, but his invitation was declined at the board meeting held on 21 January 1971. Turning down the invitation allowed Blackpool, who had just been relegated to Division Two, into the tournament. The reason for turning down the opportunity was that it was felt that the competition dates did not fit in with the various changes to the Baseball Ground in respect of new seating and refreshment areas. Blackpool went on to win the tournament and manager Bob Stokoe was grateful to Derby as they saw it as an ideal way to further their aim to regain top-flight status at the first attempt. Stokoe said, 'I shall be grateful to the Rams for a long time.'

ANGLO-ITALIAN CUP 1972/73

A further invitation was received and refused at a board meeting on 13 January 1972. Derby were still in the European Cup at this stage and had no way of knowing where this would take them in terms of the next year's pre-season arrangements. A further invitation was received for the following season, which was also declined in October 1972.

TEXACO CUP 1973/74

An invitation was declined at a board meeting on 22 June 1973.

UEFA CUP 1973/74

Top Ten in Division One

Team	P	W	D	L	F	A	W	D	L	F	A	Pts
Liverpool	42	17	3	1	45	19	8	7	6	27	23	60
Arsenal	42	14	5	2	31	14	9	6	6	26	29	57
Leeds United	42	15	4	2	45	13	6	7	8	26	32	53
Ipswich Town	42	10	7	4	34	20	7	7	7	21	25	48
Wolverhampton Wanderers	42	13	3	5	43	23	5	8	8	23	31	47
West Ham United	42	12	5	4	45	25	5	7	9	22	28	46
Derby County	42	15	3	3	43	18	4	5	12	13	36	46
Tottenham Hotspur	42	10	5	6	33	23	6	8	7	25	25	45
Newcastle United	42	12	6	3	35	19	4	7	10	25	32	45
Birmingham City	42	11	7	3	39	22	4	5	12	14	32	42

After a disappointing season in the league, the Rams had finished in seventh place, a huge fourteen points behind the champions, Liverpool. Normally a European place would have been out of reach but under the strange one city, one club rule imposed by UEFA at the time, West Ham United were ineligible. All that was needed for qualification was for Leeds United to beat Sunderland in the FA Cup final and take the Cup Winners' Cup place, freeing up a UEFA Cup spot. Unfortunately, and as we all know, Sunderland (coached by Arthur Cox at that time) pulled off a famous 1–0 victory against the red hot favourites through a magnificent shot by Ian Porterfield, so Leeds therefore took a UEFA Cup place.

UEFA Cup 1989/90

Top Ten Division One, 1988/89

Team	P	W	D	L	F	A	W	D	L	F	A	Pts
Arsenal	38	10	6	3	35	19	12	4	3	38	17	76
Liverpool	38	11	5	3	33	11	11	5	3	32	17	76
Nottingham Forest	38	8	7	4	31	16	9	6	4	33	27	64
Norwich City	38	8	7	4	23	20	9	4	6	25	25	62
Derby County	38	9	3	7	23	18	8	4	7	17	20	58
Tottenham Hotspur	38	8	6	5	31	24	7	6	6	29	22	57
Coventry City	38	9	4	6	28	23	5	9	5	19	19	55
Everton	38	10	7	2	33	18	4	5	10	17	27	54
Queens Park Rangers	38	9	5	5	23	16	5	6	8	20	21	53
Millwall	38	10	3	6	27	21	4	8	7	20	31	53

Derby had finished in fifth place at the end of the 1988/89 season, which included beating eventual champions Arsenal twice. This finish would normally have been good enough to guarantee a place in the UEFA Cup but unfortunately all English clubs were banned from European competitions following the Heysel Stadium disaster involving Liverpool fans. This was unlucky as Derby progressed very nicely under the managership of Arthur Cox and Roy McFarland and by the end of the following season owner Robert Maxwell had refused to invest any further in the club, forced the sale of star players Mark Wright and Dean Saunders to Liverpool, and Derby were relegated to Division Two.

The Stats

Top 10 Home Attendances

Season	Date	Opponent	Competition	Attendance	Result
1972/73	25/10/72	Benfica	European Cup	38,100	W 3–0
1972/73	21/3/73	Spartak Trnava	European Cup	36,472	W 2–0
1972/73	25/4/73	Juventus	European Cup	35,350	D 0–0
1975/76	22/10/75	Real Madrid	European Cup	34,839	W 4–1
1975/76	1/10/75	Slovan Bratislava	European Cup	30,888	W 3–0
1974/75	23/10/74	Atlético Madrid	UEFA Cup	29,347	D 2–2
1976/77	03/11/76	AEK Athens	UEFA Cup	28,000	L 3–2
1972/73	13/9/72	FK Željezničar	European Cup	27,350	W 2–0
1974/75	27/11/74	Velež Mostar	UEFA Cup	26,131	W 3–1
1971/72	26/4/72	Airdrieonians	Texaco Cup	25,102	W 2–1

Bottom 10 Home Attendances

Season	Date	Opponent	Competition	Attendance	Result
1994/95	15/11/94	Udinese	Anglo-Italian	1,562	W 3–1
1994/95	6/9/94	Cesena	Anglo-Italian	2,010	W 6–1
1993/94	8/9/93	Nottingham Forest	Anglo-Italian	6,654	W 3–2
1992/93	2/9/92	Notts County	Anglo-Italian	6,767	W 4–2
1992/93	8/12/92	Cremonese	Anglo-Italian	7,240	L 3–1
1992/93	11/11/92	Pisa	Anglo-Italian	8,067	W 3–0
1976/77	15/9/76	Finn Harps	UEFA Cup	13,353	W 12–0
1992/93	3/2/93	Brentford	Anglo-Italian	14,494	L 2–1
1974/75	18/9/74	Servette Geneva	UEFA Cup	17,716	W 4–1
1971/72	24/11/71	Newcastle United	Texaco Cup	20,021	W 1–0

Top 10 Away Attendances

Season	Date	Opponent	Competition	Attendance	Result
1975/76	5/11/75	Real Madrid	European Cup	120,000	L 5–1
1972/73	8/11/72	Benfica	European Cup	75,000	D 0–0
1972/73	11/4/73	Juventus	European Cup	72,000	L 3–1
1972/73	27/9/72	FK Željezničar	European Cup	60,000	W 2–1
1975/76	17/9/75	Slovan Bratislava	European Cup	45,000	L 1–0
1992/93	27/3/93	Cremonese*	Anglo-Italian	37,024	L 3–1
1971/72	8/12/71	Newcastle United	Texaco Cup	37,000	W 3–2
1974/75	6/11/74	Atlético Madrid	UEFA Cup	35,000	D 2–2
1976/77	20/10/76	AEK Athens	UEFA Cup	32,000	L 2–0
1972/73	7/3/73	Spartak Trnava	European Cup	28,000	L 1–0

* At Wembley Stadium

Bottom 10 Away Attendances

Season	Date	Opponent	Competition	Attendance	Result
1992/93	16/12/92	Reggiana	Anglo-Italian	598	W 3–0
1994/95	24/8/94	Ancona	Anglo-Italian	748	L 2–1
1994/95	5/10/94	Piacenza	Anglo-Italian	1,710	D 1–1
1976/77	29/9/76	Finn Harps	UEFA Cup	2,217	W 4–1
1993/94	31/8/93	Notts County	Anglo-Italian	3,276	L 3–2
1992/93	29/9/92	Barnsley	Anglo-Italian	3,960	W 2–1
1992/93	24/11/92	Cosenza	Anglo-Italian	4,269	W 3–0
1992/93	27/1/93	Brentford	Anglo-Italian	5,227	W 4–3
1971/72	29/9/71	Dundee United	Texaco Cup	6,000	L 3–2
1974/75	2/10/74	Servette Geneva	UEFA Cup	9,600	W 2–1

Biggest Victories

Season	Date	Opponent	Competition	Venue	Result
1976/77	15/9/76	Finn Harps	UEFA Cup	H	12–0
1994/95	6/9/94	Cesena	Anglo-Italian	H	6–1
1971/72	15/9/71	Dundee United	Texaco Cup	H	6–2
1975/76	22/10/75	Real Madrid	European Cup	H	4–1
1974/75	18/9/74	Servette Geneva	UEFA Cup	H	4–1
1976/77	29/9/76	Finn Harps	UEFA Cup	A	4–1
1972/73	25/10/72	Benfica	European Cup	H	3–0
1975/76	1/10/75	Slovan Bratislava	European Cup	H	3–0
1992/93	11/11/92	Pisa	Anglo-Italian	H	3–0
1992/93	24/11/92	Cosenza	Anglo-Italian	A	3–0
1992/93	16/12/92	Reggiana	Anglo-Italian	A	3–0

Top Goalscorers

Texaco Cup		European Cup		UEFA Cup		Anglo-Italian Cup	
John O'Hare	4	Charlie George	4	Kevin Hector	12	Paul Kitson	9
Alan Hinton	3	Kevin Hector	4	Charlie George	6	Marco Gabbiadini	6
Jim Walker	2	Francis Lee	2	Bruce Rioch	4	Mark Pembridge	5
Kevin Hector	2	Roy McFarland	2	Leighton James	3	Tommy Johnson	4

Top Appearances

Texaco Cup		European Cup		UEFA Cup		Anglo-Italian Cup	
Alan Hinton	8	Colin Boulton	12	Bruce Rioch	10	Marco Gabbiadini	12
Terry Hennessey	8	Colin Todd	12	Archie Gemmill	10	Mark Pembridge	12
Colin Boulton	8	Kevin Hector	11	Kevin Hector	9	Michael Forsyth	12
		Archie Gemmill	11	Colin Todd	9		
		Roy McFarland	11				